S. J. Celestine Edwards, S. J. Celestine Edwards

From slavery to a Bishopric

The life of Bishop Walter Hawkins of the British Methodist Episcopal Church

S. J. Celestine Edwards, S. J. Celestine Edwards

From slavery to a Bishopric
The life of Bishop Walter Hawkins of the British Methodist Episcopal Church

ISBN/EAN: 9783743451544

Manufactured in Europe, USA, Canada, Australia, Japa

Cover: Foto ©ninafisch / pixelio.de

Manufactured and distributed by brebook publishing software (www.brebook.com)

S. J. Celestine Edwards, S. J. Celestine Edwards

From slavery to a Bishopric

FROM SLAVERY TO A BISHOPRIC

OR

THE LIFE OF BISHOP WALTER HAWKINS

OF

The British Methodist Episcopal Church Canada

BY

S. J. CELESTINE EDWARDS

ASSOCIATE OF KING'S COLLEGE, LONDON; LECTURER ON CHRISTIAN
EVIDENCES; FELLOW OF THE ROYAL SOCIETY OF LITERATURE;
MEDICAL STUDENT AT THE LONDON HOSPITAL

LONDON

JOHN KENSIT, Publisher

18 PATERNOSTER, E.C.

1891

TO

WILFRED T. GRENFELL, M.R.C.S., L.R.C.P.,

Superintendent of the Deep Sea Mission,

This Work is Dedicated,

AS A TOKEN OF MANY KINDNESSES RECEIVED DURING

THE LAST FIVE YEARS,

BY

THE AUTHOR.

LIST OF WORKS CONSULTED DURING THE PREPARATION OF THIS BIOGRAPHY.

A Visit to the United States. Sturge.

Anti-Slavery days. Clark.

American System of Government.

Bancroft's History of the United States. 3 vols.

Buckingham's America. 3 vols.

Black America. W. Laird Clowes.

Constitution of the United States. Paschal.

English Nonconformity. Vaughan.

Gesta Christe. Brace.

Hosack's Law of Nations.

History of European Morals. Lecky, 2 vols.

History of the English People. Green.

History of England. Macaulay.

International Law. Gallandet.

Irving's Life of Columbus.

Life and Time of Fred. Douglas.

Men and Manners in America. 2 vols.

Power and Progress of the United States. Poussin.

Popular History of America. Mrs. Cooper.

Prescott's History of the Reign of Ferdinand and Isabella.

Robertson's America. 2 vols.

The United States. 3 vols.

The American Union. Spence.

Travels in the United States. Lady Wortley.

Willard's United States.

White, Red, and Black. 3 vols.

CONTENTS.

PREFACE.

I UNDERTAKE this work, because I think it will probably act as a stimulus to the young men of my race, who, though physically free, have not yet realised the duty they owe to themselves, and to humanity at large, and especially to the British public, to whom I feel we owe a great debt of gratitude for leading the way for our emancipation in the New World. My experience in England has led me to think that many are somewhat disappointed that the Negro, from whom they expected so much fifty or sixty years ago, has not come up to their expectations, *i.e.*, he has not improved his position quite as quickly as they feel he ought to have done. In this book I hope to set forth what Europeans well know : viz., that there is not a single nation in Europe who could have done more for itself, in the same time and under similar circumstances, than our race : they have expected too much of us, with far less opportunities. Besides, it is all very well to tell people what they ought to do, but it is quite another thing to give them the opportunity of doing.

1st. We cannot expect much from a people who had to start an existence upon nothing, like the West Indian Negroes.

2nd. Neither can we hope for much progress from any nation who are treated as our race have been, and are being treated, since the American Civil War. And

3rd. No nation can be expected to advance in so-called civilisation whose faults are continually being paraded before them, as ours are in the literature of the superior race. It is well known, and most keenly felt, in every country where the Negro has been sent as an exile, that his superior brethren have used every means and meanness, not only to make him feel his position, but to prolong his degradation, and even to discourage any and every attempt on the part of the Negro to approach the social equality of the most abandoned white man. Our own conviction is that until the Negro knows and is convinced in head and heart that God has not sent him into the world as a mere toy to be kicked about by every and any one—until he learns that fate has not made him to be a mere spectator and serf— we can never hope for better things to befall our people. Our aim in this book is not merely to give an account of one of our own kind, or to turn the light of this closing century upon slavery, but to put into the hands of the rising generation the history of one who has, by sheer force of character, raised himself above the degrading condition of the life in which he was born.

By following Walter Hawkins from a slave farm to a Bishopric, we shall see how Providence has provided every man with the means—if he will use them—to improve his position in the world; the young Negro will see that while he may not become a bishop, doctor, or lawyer, he may so utilise his opportunities that he shall command respect from those who have hitherto regarded all Negroes as vagrants, destined to wander on the face of the earth. The race will feel that, with patience, perseverance, and hard work, what Bishop Hawkins has done in one direction, millions may do in other ways. Ah! we trust that his life will urge the race not to look to others so much as to themselves. I confess my inability to do justice to the subject, as I have had no experience in this kind of work; and, secondly, I have had little time to give to its preparation, as I have to work for my living while prosecuting my studies. I have tried to give an historical sketch of slavery from its introduction in the New World down to the time of Bishop Hawkins. I have also tried to give an historical sketch of several places where he stopped before he finally settled in Canada, as I thought it would add to the interest of the life of one who has served his race—and through them humanity—in a way I should like to serve them.

I must thank my many friends for their advice and suggestions. I do hope, most sincerely, that no one will blame Bishop Hawkins for any statement which they might think ought to have been left out. Perhaps a little more polish would have made me choose better words to express myself; still I will trust to the generosity of the impartial reader to exonerate me from any wilful desire to wound the susceptibility of the race who are, for the most part, responsible for our shortcomings.

S. J. CELESTINE EDWARDS.

South Hackney,
London, N.E., 1891.

INTRODUCTION.

No race under heaven (except, perhaps, the Jewish nation) have suffered so many wrongs, endured more insults, and survived so many centuries of private and public vicissitudes as the African race. Many of the nations who afflicted the African are no more; yet, at this day, the nations who glory in the knowledge of their being members of the Aryan family, or some other real or imaginary race, take a pride in perpetually reminding the Negro of the inferiority of his kind: that he is a savage, or at least a child, who does not improve in intelligence, though he develops in body. Every nation of antiquity have had something to say in praise or blame of the Negro, and most, if not all, have had something to do with him. By all, ancient and modern, he has been robbed, murdered and enslaved; his daughter has been robbed of her virtue before his eyes; his home broken, and his country pillaged and laid waste. It is as yesterday that the nations of the West began to think seriously either of his country or the Negro,

or both ; but none of the ancients ever afflicted
the man as the moderns have done.   Not content
with setting tribe against tribe in Africa, they tore
him away from the bosom of his country ; packed
him in ships, chained as though he were a murderer,
and sold him.   They were not content with these
methods of degrading him, but every moral, mental
and religious influence was kept from him—for
centuries—save such as would tend to make him
more docile to his master.   Everything was done to
completely crush the moral sense out of the man, and,
as if all this loathsome treatment would not serve
their purpose, historians and travellers, until late
years, misrepresented him.   Some even went as far
as to say that his skull was too thick for culture—
rather a sad reflection on the Being or Power that
called him into being.   Believers in the Bible
held that he was born to serve his brethren.
Evolutionists maintained that there was only a
step between him and the ape.   Men of every
profession have found fault with the Negro for his
indolence, while priding themselves on superior
virtues ; nothing was too bad to say of him, even
when the Negro rose above the condition in which
might and superior craft had placed him.   The
Negro even now is only known as a " nigger ".
He is shouted at in the most enlightened cities in
the world as a " darkey," " nigger," " Sambo,"

etc.   If he appears respectable, every effort is made in the United States to keep him down. The whites do not hesitate to say that "quashey" is only fit to be a hewer of wood and drawer of water; no matter how well he is educated or how clean his body, he must not sit next to the most degraded white man.   Sometimes in a tram; at other times in a train; if he goes to the theatre, he must sit where all blacks are sitting.   They will neither shave him nor serve him in a dram shop. In the church, where people are supposed to worship one God, the Negro cannot find a seat. When he was a slave he could cook the food and serve at the table; but now he is free he must not eat in the same room as the white man.   The poor innocent child cannot be comfortable in the school where the white children are, no matter how much tax his father pays to the State; hence he must have his own church and chapel—except Roman Catholic—his own shaving and drinking saloon.   In many of the States even the right of citizenship is denied him.   Whatever crime he commits is too often magnified an hundred fold; and, when he is wronged, justice is withheld from him in courts of law for no other reason than that he is a Negro.   Very often his greatest oppressors are men who have been forced to flee their own country by want or crime.   There is a saying in

the Southern States : " When the nigger is down
keep him down, for when the nigger rises, hell
rises"; and the whites seem to act very much on
that principle.   In the old days, though some ac-
knowledged that " many of the Negroes possess a
natural goodness of heart and warmth of affection,"
yet they used to fix their prices not merely according
to their bodily powers, but in proportion to the
docility and good disposition of their commodity ;
so at this very time, while they are patronising
the Negro and professing friendliness towards him,
every artifice is being used to stop his growth in
the United States.   Under the pretext of kindly
feeling he is told to go out of the country.   If the
Negro should ask : " Where ? " he is told : " Go
back to your fatherland, or anywhere, so long as
you go ".   The Negro might well reply : " 1st. I
did not come here by choice : you stole me from
my country ; you made money out of my degradation, blood and bones.   2nd. The country out of
which you are sending me is no more yours than
mine : white men came here because they were
driven from Europe by tyranny and poverty ; and
you no sooner landed than you began to murder
(in cold blood) the Indians, and plundered Africa
to enrich yourselves, and built an empire ; so that
if you think that might is right I don't.   3rd.
Moreover, your race have divided Africa among

themselves, and call it theirs. Don't you think that they ought to clear out in order that we might go in? And do you suppose that we can go out of your (so-called) country without your paying us our due? You have got a large indemnity to pay for the Negroes whom you threw overboard to lighten the cargo of your slave ships; for those whom you killed under the lash, chased to death by bloodhounds, and caused to perish in the slave-gang. What about the pay for nigh three hundred years of free labour? What about our property? And surely if all my race were willing to go, and you had removed every barrier in Africa, you will certainly have to find us a free and comfortable passage back, for we would not think of going as you brought us." We know it will be argued that the Negro has improved by being a slave. A few may have improved their condition—which was due, not to the generosity of slave-holders, but in spite of them—and the majority have paid enormously for it. Just think what it must mean to a nation who were instructed into the vices of a foreign power, and not many, or very little, of its virtues. To keep a man a slave, means a sacrifice of all his moral qualities. Courage, singleness of affection, gentleness and parental attachment were all offered up on the auction-block and the lash. The common decency which the Negro in his savage condition regarded was abused by slavery. Men, women and children were thrown together. Marriage was unknown. We wonder a race did tolerate such iniquities from men viler than themselves. Still the Negro has outlived the ravages on his oppression, barbarity of his master, and will outlive the prejudices of to-day. In spite of his forcible removal from the land of his nativity, and in spite of all the difficulties of his forced condition, he increases and multiplies in every country whither he has been taken. And now the Negro has come through many vicissitudes to be a real political force in the world. At first he was pitied; now the Yankee begins to fear his number. We do not think any one of us need be alarmed about what Mr. Froude has had to say. We have outlived his master's hatred of our race; and we sincerely trust that in time the Negro will show the world that he is "worthier of regard and stronger, than the colour of his kind". Whatever other races may think about our future destiny, the Negro himself is very hopeful; we shall plod on and wait. The opening up of Africa, from whatever motives, is doing us and the nations good. The growing increase of the Negro population of the United States, Canada, the West Indies and South America are forces which are acting upon the minds of our late masters with a certain amount of alarm. The spread of education among our race is enabling us to know what the white people have thought of us, and what they are now thinking. All these things will work wonders in our minds, and will tend to help us to shape our future course. We contemplate neither war nor bloodshed to gain our end : ours shall be a victory of peace, for " Peace hath her victories no less renowned than war ". It is a long process ; but it is a sure and sound policy. All other races have had, or are having, their day : ours is coming, when those who despised, degraded and abused us in our childish innocence shall know, that the Negro is a rational individual, composed of mind and body, of outward and inward being, of necessity and freedom like themselves—though to himself a mystery, to the ignorant a laughing-stock, and to philosophers the subject of speculation ; yet to the world of spirits he is an object of deepest thought, of God's Almightiness, wisdom and love, a living witness veiled round by a black skin. He sees God at a distance, yet he is as certain of His existence and justice as the One Eternal Righteous Spirit as he is of his own. The Negro feels that he is a child of revelation—weak yet strong, poor, but rich in the faith ; that, by patience and works, justice cannot long be withheld from his race.

CHAPTER I.

HISTORICAL SKETCH—SLAVERY.

"BANISHMENT is but the change of place," said Seneca, "and this blessing we owe to the Almighty Power—call it what you will—either God or an incorporeal Reason—a Divine Spirit or Fate, and the unchangeable course of causes and effects. It is, however, so ordered that nothing can be taken from us but what we can spare, and that which is most magnificent and valuable continues with us. Wherever we go, we have the heavens over our heads, and no farther from us than they were before ; and so long as we can entertain our eyes and thoughts with these glories, what matters it what ground we tread?" This might be aptly applied to our race, who had no choice in their banishment from the Fatherland. The discovery of the West Indies by Columbus, and America by Cabot and Vespucci, drew the attention of Europe from domestic slumber to the New World, concerning the existence of which Europeans were, for the most part, sceptical. Not only a New World; but there was on the virgin soil a race of people who appeared to the Spaniards as an idle and improvident race, indifferent to most of the objects of human anxiety and comfort. Amid the region of the Vega the encircling seasons

I

brought them its stores of fruit, when some were
ripening on their boughs, crops were being gathered
in their full maturity from the fields—some trees bud-
ding into new life, while others blossomed into bloom,
giving promise of still succeeding abundance.

What need, then, were there for the childlike natives
to garner up, and anxiously provide for, coming days,
when nature lavished their lands so abundantly?
Theirs was a perpetual harvest.   To men who lived in
such abundance, what need of toiling, spinning, or
labouring throughout the year, when neither nature nor
custom prescribed the necessity of better clothing than
the former herself supplied?   Wherever the European
went among these—children of the wood—it was a
continual scene of festivities, and a constant stream of
rejoicing ; while the natives hastened from all parts to
lay the treasures of their groves, streams, and mountains at the feet of beings whom they ignorantly
thought had fallen from the skies to bring blessings
to their country.   We would that it were so ; but the
strangers betrayed their confidence, and proved themselves rather to have ascended from the abyss, bringing curses not blessings.   As long as Isabella lived,
the Indians found an efficient friend and protector ;
but " her death," says the Venerable Las Casas, " was
the signal for their destruction ".   " Immediately on
that event . . . Columbus, who seems to have had
no doubt, from the first, of the Crown's absolute
right of property over the natives, carried it to its
full extent in the colonies.   Every Spaniard, how-

ever humble, had his proportion of slaves ; and men, many of them not only incapable of estimating the awful responsibility of the situation, but without the least touch of humanity in their natures, were individually entrusted with unlimited power, of the disposal of the lives and destinies of their fellow-creatures. They abused this trust in the grossest manner ; tasking the unfortunate Indian far beyond his strength, inflicting the most refined punishments on the indolent and hunting down those who resisted or escaped like so many beasts of chase, with ferocious bloodhounds.

" Every step of the white man's progress in the New World may be said to have been on the corpse of a native. Faith is staggered by the recital of the number of victims immolated in these fair regions within a very few years after the discovery ; and the heart sickens at the loathsome details of barbarities, recorded by one who, if his sympathies have led him sometimes to overcolour, can never be suspected of wilfully misstating facts of which he was an eyewitness."* On the northern coast of South America —Terra Firma, as it was called in contrast with the islands—when it had been explored, and before its virgin soil had been polluted by the touch of selfish and self-seeking plunderers, it occurred to the ardent imaginative mind of Las Casas that a colony might be founded, in which Spaniards might exercise a sort of paternal rule over the gentle natives, whose

* Prescott's *History of Ferdinand and Isabella.*

hospitality was evinced towards Columbus and his fol-
lowers, in a marked manner, and to prove to the other
settlers—whose avarice, pride, and sordid care had
been made manifest in the paradise of the Indians
—that the two races could live together and mingle
with mutual profit.　With this notion Las Casas
undertook to select fifty men of upright character,
who would advance the principle of equity in dealing
with the natives, and make it their serious purpose to
draw them by lawful means to the belief in the Gospel.
To distinguish his men from the other Spaniards, they
were to wear a white dress, with a coloured cross upon
it, and to proclaim as widely as possible that their
mission was one of peace.　Within the limits of the
proposed colony, slavery was to be forbidden.

In his anxiety to lighten the expense of the colony
and to procure revenue to the Crown, Columbus had
recommended that the natives of the West Indies—
being cannibal and ferocious invaders of their peaceful
neighbours—should be captured and sold as slaves,
or exchanged with merchants for live stock, and other
necessary supplies.　This was in the year 1493.

According to Las Casas, the Indians were to be
won by presents to friendly relation with the colonists,
and then hired to cultivate the soil for wages as free
men.　For himself, he asked for nothing except the
right of selecting the men with whom he should try
his experiment, liberty to advise freely and to exercise a regulating power over the colony along with the
civil officers to be appointed by the Crown.　Though

prompted by the best motives, Las Casas knew from experience that no royal sanction could be secured for any scheme of colonisation which did not promise some return to the revenue. Therefore, to satisfy this demand, and to save the lives of the natives, whom he passionately loved, he, in a moment of weakness, proposed that every one of his fifty settlers—whom he thought were as unselfish as himself—should have licence to buy three Negroes, with permission to increase the number to ten by the consent of the Protector.

Evidently Las Casas thought that these Negroes were a stronger and hardier race than the Indians, and would share the toil and bear some of the heavier burdens of the natives in tilling the ground, etc. But the plan of this illustrious man never came to maturity; and not a single Negro was bought or sold under this clause in the charter. Moreover, he afterwards saw the folly of the scheme, and confessed it, saying: "I forgot for the moment that the sellers were menstealers". Las Casas was not the first to introduce Negro slavery in the New World, as they must have been on the spot for him to suggest their purchase; in any case, we have no authentic date until 1503, when the first ship-load of Negroes was landed in the island of St. Domingo. The impossibility of effecting any improvement in the New World, unless the Spanish planters could command the labour of the natives, was an insuperable objection to Las Casas's plan. In order to overcome this difficulty, the Spaniards purchased a number of Negroes from the Portuguese settlement on the coast of Africa. In 1503 only a few Negroes were brought into the West Indies ; but, in 1511, we find that Ferdinand permitted the importation of a greater number.

1st. Because they were proved to be more robust and hardier than the natives. 2nd. They were more capable of enduring fatigue, and more patient under servitude. 3rd. And that the labour of one Negro was thought to be equal to that of four Indians.

In vain did Cardinal Ximenes protest "against the iniquity of reducing one race of men to slavery, while endeavouring to save the lives and restoring the liberty of another". Charles V. granted a patent to one of his Flemish favourites, by which he had the exclusive right to import four thousand Negroes to the New World. This man sold his patent to some Genoese merchants for 25,000 ducats, who degraded commerce by bringing a larger number of slaves than ever had been introduced before in the West Indies. From that time the traffic extended with alarming rapidity to the continent of America. The Africans, who were carried to the western world were, as a general rule, of the weakest of the people in their own country : people who did not fairly represent the best qualities and endowments of the race—even the traditions of their country were carried away in the most distorted form. They were for the most part people from the alluvial districts of Africa, who had been preyed upon by local diseases, and captives taken in those tribal wars which devastated large towns and villages in the heart of the country, and *is* until this day. The more powerful tribes pushed the weaker ones from the abundant supplies of food—from the high lands to the sea coast—whither the white man either stole, bribed, or made war against them. They did not even scruple to call in the aid of the rum bottle, and every other unrighteous means, in order to entrap them to supply the slave market. Nevertheless, some of the better class and stalwart sons of Africa found themselves as slaves among the rabble. Hundreds of tribes were mixed together in the slave markets of the New World. The nefarious traffic in human flesh, which began in the midst of pestilence, war, and famine, soon pushed these Negroes beneath the physical standard of the hardier tribes of Africa; and the common moral standard of the human species, with which they were surrounded in their new home —the galling bond of slavery—bound their bodies, and fettered their intellectual faculties, impaired their social affection, and reduced them to move like common machines. The atrocious debasement of slavery paralysed their reflective faculty, suspended their judgment, so that their power of choice was nil; while reason and conscience had little influence over their conduct. Being governed by fear, the Negro became a mere automaton in the hands of his master.

About one hundred and sixteen years after the Portuguese took the first few Negroes to the West Indies we find a slaver landing some slaves in Virginia (*i.e.*, 1619) in exchange for food to relieve the hunger of some famishing sailors. Better for those Negroes had they been eaten, rather than to have been enslaved, that others might eat. But the African was not alone ; as it was a common thing at this time to send white men into servitude—being sent out as convicts from England, some of whom afterwards became masters, others slave-drivers. Thus the reader will readily understand how it was that they inflicted such dreadful punishment upon the Negro, as we shall hereafter mention.

" Virginia was the mother of slavery in America, as well as 'the mother of Presidents,' unfortunate for her, unfortunate for the other colonies, and thrice unfortunate for the poor, weak, and friendless Negroes who, from 1619 to 1863, were made to yield their liberty, their toil, their bodies, and their intellects to a system which ground them to powder. While it thus affected the Africans, the white man and institutions felt the direful influence of slavery, for it touched the brightest features of social life, and they faded under the contact of its poisonous breath. It affected legislation, local and national ; it made and destroyed statesmen ; it prostrated and bullied honest public sentiment ; it strangled the voice of the press, while it awed the pulpit into silent acquiescence ; it organised the judiciary of the States, and wrote decisions of judges ; it gave States their political being, and afterwards dragged them by the forehair through the stormy sea of a civil war ; laid the parricidal fingers of treason against the fair throat of liberty : and through all time to come no event will be more sincerely deplored than the introduction of slavery into the colony of Virginia.* In degrading the Negro, the Virginian colonists did not fail to degrade themselves. How could it be otherwise? Can a man use pitch without smearing himself? Alas! for Virginia—better far had thy virgin soil remained untouched than that thou shouldst have witnessed the loud sad wails of agony sent up from the broken hearts of the sons of Africa, into whose mouths Burns put the following lines :—

It was in sweet Senegal that my foes did me enthral
   For the lands of Virginia—ginia, O ;
Torn from that lovely shore, and never to see it more,
   And, alas! I am weary, weary, O.

All on that charming coast is no bitter snow and frost
   Like the lands of Virginia—ginia, O ;
There streams for ever flow, and there flowers for ever blow,
   And, alas! I am weary, weary, O.

The burden I must bear, while the cruel scourge I fear
   In the lands of Virginia—ginia, O ;
And I think on my friends most dear, with the bitter, bitter
    tear,
   And, alas! I am weary, weary, O.

It appears, however, that Virginia began to repent of her iniquity in 1776, for William Gordon of Roxburgh, Mass., wrote: " The Virginians begin their declaration of rights by saying that ' all men are born equally free and independent; and have certain interests, and

---

* Williams' *History of the Negro Race in America.*

natural rights, of which they cannot by any compact deprive themselves or their posterity, among which are their enjoyments of life and *liberty* '. The Congress declare that they ' hold these truths to be self-evident, that all men are created *equal*, that they are endowed by their Creator with certain INALIENABLE RIGHTS—that among these are life, *liberty*, and pursuit of happiness '."

Maryland, the State in which the Bishop was born, constituted a part, and was for a long time within the limits, of the colony of Virginia, consequently the slave traffic of the latter extended throughout the entire territory. Here the colonists found the soil rich ; and the cultivation of tobacco would be a profitable enterprise. The country was new, and, the physical obstacles in the way of the advancement of civilisation being numerous and formidable, the demand for robust labourers became an absolute necessity ; and, as Negroes were at hand and cheap, there was nothing to do but import them. Thus, in 1671, the legislature passed "an act encouraging the importation of Negroes and slaves," *i.e.*, Negroes and white convicts. The former were "used to till the soil, fell trees, assist mechanics, and to man light crafts along the water-ways". Steadily Africans found their way into houses of opulence and refinement, either on account of novelty or cheapness, or both. This gave rise to an import tax being imposed upon slaves imported into the colony, which did not destroy the vile traffic, but supplied grist to the government's mill. In 1696 an act was passed laying " an imposition on the slaves and white persons imported into the colony ". Mr. Williams explains that " the word 'imported' means persons who could not pay their passage, and were therefore indentured to the master of the vessel. When they arrived their time was hired out, if they were free, for a term of years at so much per year ; but, if they were slaves, the buyer had to pay all claims against this species of property before he could acquire a fee-simple in the slave."[*]

In 1704 the legislature passed another act " imposing threepence per gallon on rum, wine, brandy, and spirits ; twenty shillings per poll for Negroes, for raising a supply to defray the public charge in this province ; and twenty shillings per poll on Irish servants, to prevent the importation of too great a number of Irish papists into this province " : which act was passed for only " three years "; but the hell-conceived child, avarice, kept it alive with all its hideousness for twenty-one years. Rum, slavery, and bigotry were the forces which prompted the colonial economists of that day to stain the statute-book with such a vile law—depraved sentiments made law, and law fashioned slaves and servants into chattelled goods. Poor wooden-headed law-makers! knew ye not that the very law which ye made to keep your nests well-feathered would dehumanise and make you cruel tyrants? Ill-got fortune can never make villains re-

---

[*] *History of the Negro Race in America*, p. 242.

spectable. The dignity of labour was dishonoured by your ill-conceived enactments; while a remorseless greed for wealth created, perpetuated, and deluged the country with a thirst for the blood of the innocent for gain. Few people at this day can picture to themselves the horrors of the slave traffic at that time, and long after. Masters were men who believed that the wretched slaves were indispensable to the property of the country—convicts, whose moral sense was already deadened by the crimes which caused them to be transported; men, whose religion was a mere name, whose moral sensibilities were numbed by their frequent acts of vice, and whose god was their passions, could not be expected to be humane. In fact, they were mostly members of the criminal class— " people whose blood might have been traced through many generations of stupid, sluggish, and vicious ancestors, with no claim to merit but the names they bore ". Indeed, such was the character of these " scoundrels " that the best colonists dreaded their continual increase, and well they might, when the " age revolted at the idea of going back to such as these for the roots of a genealogical tree ". Here is a letter from one of these refuse of Europe, or his representative, taken from the *Maryland Gazette* of July 30, 1767 : " I confess I am one who think a young country cannot be settled, cultivated, and improved without people of some sort; and that it is much better for the country to receive convicts than slaves. The wicked and bad amongst them that come into

this province mostly run away to the northward, mix
with their people, and pass for honest men; while
those more innocent, and who came for very small
offences, serve their time out here, behave well, and
become useful people." This convict, or otherwise,
even estimated " that, for these last thirty years—
communibus annis—there have been at least 600 convicts per year imported into this province, and these
have probably gone into 400 families ". Alas! for
Maryland and for the poor African slave. Was it likely
that people of the criminal class, so *far* removed from
social and moral influence, and from all restraint, at a
time when it was necessary for detectives to dog their
every step in Europe—when there were no steamships
crossing the Atlantic in seven days—when there was
no electric telegraph, and the quickest passage took
months — that these convicts would be transformed
into angelic masters?

" Who but a man swayed with the most sordid selfish-
ness would endeavour," cried one of the colonists, " to
disarm the people of the colony of all caution against
imminent danger, lest their just apprehensions should
interfere with his little scheme of profit? And who
but such a man would appear publicly as an advocate
for the importation of felons, the scouring of jails, and
the abandoned outcasts of the British nation, as a
mode in any sort eligible for peopling a young
country?"

These were the creatures who undoubtedly
became, for the most part, masters and slave-

drivers in the terrible days which followed:
felons and convicts, with hearts like flint, hardened
in the furnace of crimes, let loose unrestrained, and
given over to unbridled passions and lusts. It is this
convict element which, through its numerous and
ever-increasing popularity, created and inflamed
popular sentiment in favour of an indiscriminate
and cruel code of laws for the brutal government of
Negro slavery. The pride of the revolting convict
stunted every humane instinct in his nature, so that
the African's helpless and dying appeal for mercy and
kindness never moved him, except in the direction of
making him feel his burden the more. These masters
and Negro-drivers were considered by their contemporaries as "guilty of the most shameful misrepre-
sentation and the grossest calumny upon the whole
province, and the most abandoned profligates in the
universe". Who, then, can wonder at their harsh
treatment of the Negro?—whom these convicts hated,
not because of his condition or circumstance, but on
account of his barbaric nationality and colour. Thus,
to make him feel more keenly his master's contempt and hatred, convicts no longer called the
African a Negro, but "nigger"—so using the Negro to
divert the attention of the virtuous colonists, who
despised their pedigree, from their hateful selves.
The convict class of Maryland had the honour to
make a slave code, which, for barbarity and general
inhumanity, has no equal—except in South Carolina—
in the annals of American slavery.

1st. In 1723 they made " an act to prevent tumultu-
ous meetings and other irregularities of Negroes
and other slaves," no matter for what purpose
these meetings were held. They were to have
their ears " cropt, on order of justice ". What
known and untold wrongs have been committed
in the name, and under the pretext of doing
" justice " ! What sense of justice had these
transported convicts ?

2nd. The Negro was denied the right of possessing
property—not even an ass—like one of those
who voted for such a law.

3rd. The act gave authority to any white man to
kill a Negro who resisted an attempt to arrest
him. If such authority had been given to the
constables of England before these convicts
were transported, there would not have been
sufficient voting convicts left to carry such a
clause.

In 1751 the act of 1723 was supplemented in the
master's favour, so that, if he were killed in taking the
Negro, the legislature handed a sum of money to his
relations. To crown their abominable enactments,
and rob the Negro of the last vestige of the rights of
manhood, an act was passed by which it was made
legal " not to hang a Negro " by the neck, but " his
body was quartered and exposed to public view ".
Having augmented the fortune of his master, a respectable man sometimes thought fit to reward his old
slave by giving him his freedom in his old age, or make

provision in his will, that at his death his slave or slaves should be emancipated. Again the Negro-hating convicts stepped in and forbade manumission by the last will and testament. From the introduction of slavery until 1780 Maryland, as we now know it, was stricken with silence in the face of the monstrous and stubborn slave traffic—the press was gagged, the men of God were struck with dumbness, and states-men like dead fishes went with the stream. It was not until men like Jefferson exclaimed : "That throughout the whole commerce, master and slave, is a perpetual exercise of the most boisterous passions, the most unrelenting despotism on the one part and degrading submission on the other," that a ray of hope began to shine through the dark horizon of "Black America". "Our children see this," said Jefferson, "and learn to imitate it—for man is an imitative animal. This quality is the germ of all education to him. From his cradle to his grave he is learning to do what he sees others do. If a parent could find no motive, either in his philanthropy or his self-love, for restraining the intemperance of passion towards his slave, it should always be a sufficient one that his child is present. But it is not generally sufficient. The parent storms ; the child looks on, catches the lineaments of wrath, puts on some airs in the circle of smaller slaves, gives a loose tongue to the worst of passions, and, thus nursed, educated, and daily exercised in tyranny, cannot but be stamped with odious peculiarities. The man must be a prodigy who

can retain his manners and morals undepraved by
such circumstances. And with what execration
should the statesman be loaded who, permitting one
half the citizens thus to trample on the rights of the
other, transforms those into despots and these into
enemies, destroys the morals of the one part and the
amor patriae of the other?" In 1706 a society was
formed at Trenton, New Jersey, for "the Abolition of
Slavery". The Quakers set the example to Christian
America by emancipating their slaves. Anti-slavery
societies sprang up in almost every State; in vain did
loud-mouthed pulpit orators of the ex-convict type try to
prop up the traffic as a divine institution, when such
men as Dr. Franklin threw in his lot with the abolitionists and charged the enemies of liberty. In 1789
. he wrote : "Slavery is such an atrocious debasement
of human nature that its very extirpation, if not performed with solicitous care, may sometimes open a
source of serious evils". Ever year, from the first
formation of an anti-slavery society down to Garrison,
was crowned with success; his efforts were untiring,
and his method of attacking the traffic was unique.
"I determined," said he, "at every hazard to lift up
the standard of emancipation in the eyes of the nation,
within sight of Bunker's Hill and in the birthplace of
liberty. That standard is now unfurled, and long may
it float unhurt by the spoilations of time or the missiles
of a desperate foe ; yea, till every chain is broken and
every bondman set free ! Let southern oppression
tremble ; let their secret abettors tremble ; let all the

enemies of the persecuted black tremble. . . . On this question my influence, humble as it is, is felt at this moment to a considerable extent; and it shall be felt in coming years—not perniciously, but beneficially, not as a curse, but as a blessing—and posterity will bear testimony that I was right. I desire to thank God that He enables me to disregard the fear of man, which bringeth a snare, and speak truth in its simplicity and power; and I here close with this dedication :—

> Oppression! I have seen thee face to face,
> And met thy cruel eye and cloudy brow
> By the soul-withering glance. I fear not now,
> For dread to prouder feelings doth give place,
> Of deep abhorrence, scorning the disgrace
> Of slavish knees that at thy footstool bow;
> I also kneel—but with far other vow
> Do hail thee and thy herd of hirelings base;
> I swear, while life-blood warms my throbbing veins,
> Still to oppose and thwart, with heart and hand,
> Thy brutalising sway—till Afric's chains
> Are burst, and freedom rules the rescued land,
> Trampling oppression and his iron rod;
> Such is the vow I take—so help me, God!

"Well done, thou prophet of the living God! Millions of Negroes bless thee and thine for all the energy which thou in thy glorious day did put forth!" Time would fail us to name the illustrious men and women who helped, both in England and America, to bring about the abolition of Negro slavery. Yet it must not be thought that these illustrious men were the first to express anti-slavery sentiments; for the Mosaic law pronounced death upon the manstealer. Zeno, the founder of Stoicism, laid down the principle that " all men are equal, and that virtue alone establishes a difference between them ". Anti-slavery sentiment was eloquent in the days of Christ, who Himself laid it down as a fundamental principle of the new religion that " whatsoever ye would that men should do unto you, do ye even so to them ". Seneca taught the slave-holders of his time to " let your slaves laugh, or talk, or keep silence in your presence, as in that of the father of the family. Remember that he whom you call your slave belongs to the same race as yourself. Will you despise a man for circumstances which may become your own ? We all have one common origin, and no other is nobler than another unless he is more ready for good deeds." That God-given mandate quoted above carried the gospel of humanity into the palaces of the Cæsars and Antonies. In 312 A.D. a law was passed under Constantine the Great condemning the poisoning of a slave, or tearing his body with the nails of a wild beast, or branding him to be homicide. In 314 A.D. liberty was declared a right which could not be taken away. Sixty years of captivity could not take from the free-born the right of demanding liberty. In 316 Constantine wrote to an archbishop : " It has pleased me for a long time to establish that, in the Christian Church, masters can give liberty to their slaves, provided they do it in the presence of all the assembled people and with the assistance of Christian priests, and that, in order to preserve the memory of the fact, some written document should inform where they sign as parties or as witnesses"; and in 321 A.D. Constantine directed that "he who under a religious feeling has given a just liberty to his slaves in the bosom of the Christian Church will be thought to have made a gift of a right similar to Roman citizenship, which privilege was only granted to those who emancipate under the eyes of the priest".*

Chrysostom, the golden-mouth, who advised Vespasian to restore the republic, exhorted Trajan to devote himself to the welfare of his subjects, and imitate God in philanthropy, as well as those in which he proclaimed to the common people, who were his favourite auditors, the dignity of labour, the sin of slavery and the folly of training hermits. St. Theodore of Constantinople ventured to put forth the command : "Thou shalt possess no slave, neither for domestic purposes nor for the labour of the fields, for man is made in the image of God". (*Vide Gesta Christi.*)

The opposition of slavery shook the thrones of Europe during medieval times. In 441 A.D. a church council (Orange) enacted that a slave once emancipated in Church could not be made either slave or serf again without incurring ecclesiastical censures. The Justiman Code bristles with enactments against slavery. From Emperor Leo, 717 A.D., we find an unbroken stream of sentiments shaping law both for the amelioration of slaves and the suppression thereof. Thirty-

---

* *Vide* Lecky, *History of European Morals*, vol. ii. p. 62.

seven church councils are reported to have passed acts favourable to slaves. One council called in London by Anselm forbade absolutely the nefarious business of selling human beings like brute beasts. Sir Thomas Smith, who was a statesman in the time of Elizabeth, 1570, said : "That already in his time slaves were unknown in England, and of serfs only a few survived, but that both conditions were recognised in English law. I think both in France and England the change of religion to the more gentle and more equal sort (as the Christian religion is in respect to the Gentiles) caused this whole kind of servile servitude and slavery to be brought into that moderation, so that they almost extinguished the whole." Austria and France led the way, and finally slavery was driven out of Europe, never to appear again.

Then it found a home in the New World, but not even there could the wretch find rest for the sole of its feet, for in 1688 the "Friends" of Pennsylvania publicly protested against it, while the Roman Catholics hunted down the monster in the West Indies, as we have elsewhere shown ; the work steadily went on until England could not endure the united efforts of Wilberforce and his stalwart co-workers, but yielded up the iniquitous system on the 29th of July, 1833, leaving America and the Americans to struggle on, though Jefferson had told his countrymen : "Indeed, I tremble for my country when I reflect that God is just, that His justice cannot sleep for ever". At last this prophetic declaration was fulfilled, and the down-trodden Negro took up arms and stood side by side with those heroic white men who were prepared to fight for the absolute emancipation of the people, God be thanked! We only regret that statesmen with the spirit of Franklin, Rush, Hamilton, and Jay; that divines like Hopkins, Edwards, Channing, and Stiles; philanthropists like Lundy, Woolman, and Garrison are not now moving among the Americans to crown the labours of those illustrious dead, by removing those obstacles which are second to slavery in importance. Alas! for the proud republic whose constitution is supposed to be founded upon "Liberty". Let America, in the fulness of her pride, wave on high in her banner fraternity and liberty, if not equality, to each of her subjects. Let America learn from most of the European powers that virtue, not colour, makes the man.

> Then let us pray that come it may,
> As come it will for a' that;
> That man to man the world o'er
> Shall brothers be for a' that.

As sure as the day star of human liberty has arisen above the dark horizon of slavery, so assuredly will the sun of righteousness penetrate the black cloud of prejudice against the Negro, and shine in majestic splendour to the glory of God, and the peaceful dwelling together of the races which have made the United States what she is. Let Americans remember that the Negro helped to fight for her independence under the slave-holder Washington, and fought gloriously in the Civil War. Remember, too, that they helped to augment the wealth of your boasted republic. We do not ask that her government should create right, but to protect them, as we are not now ignorant that governments are instituted to maintain order, secure peace, administer justice, and protect the rights of all people, and not to destroy or diminish them. We do not ask the United States' Government to enlarge the rights of the Negro by contracting the rights of the white man in order to equalise either property, social position, or political power. We know that such an act would involve the infringement and contraction of their rights. We know too that—

> Order is heaven's first law, and thus confess'd,
> Some are, and must be, greater than the rest;
> More rich, more wise; but who infers from hence
> That such are happier shocks common-sense.
> —Pope.

Thus, we only demand justice for our race, a right which the constitution affirms in the following terms : " All citizens of each State shall be entitled to all the privileges and immunities of citizens in the several States," and as long as she withholds a little of the rights which this and other sections of the constitution allow, so long we will persist in making our demand. Why should our race contribute to the maintenance of the government in the shape of taxes when black children are kicked out of State schools ? Why should a Negro be punished if he breaks the law, and a white man go free when he does the same ? Is not a government impotent when it cannot protect the weak and promote the welfare of all citizens? If a government is based upon popular and democratic principles as that of the United States, is it not its duty to protect the weak elector, and punish those who use force to prevent some citizens from using their electoral rights? In Great Britain and Ireland the most ignorant and unlettered farm labourer who is a lodger or householder can vote, but in the United States the Negro, because he has been a slave, too often cannot do so. Which then is the freest country, and in which have the subjects the most liberty? Where is the protection for the respectable Negro citizen in a tram, train, or 'bus in the U.S.A.? The Negro does not beg for pity or favour; he merely asks for more of justice, and less of either. Let the United or any other State withhold justice as long as it likes from the weaker members of the community, the day will come when those very people will rise either by craft or force, or both, and have it. What people could have been more oppressed than the Frenchmen of the preceding two centuries? From the most servile deference to monarchy, men passed at once to a democracy of a bolder character than either the Greek or the United States' republics. They sprang from a gradation of ranks which rose tier upon tier, assigning to the upper class special privileges, and heaping on the lower orders penalties and fiscal burdens. The nation dropped into a level on which all citizens were equal. God forbid that the Negro problem should bring such

a calamity upon America as the French Revolution !
But the more a people suffer the more revengeful will
they become, when they get the opportunity. Let
America remember that the marvellous revolution of
opinion which produced such an upheaval was not the
growth of a few years, but a power that was long brewing.
The Negroes may yet have their Voltaires and Rosseaus
to kindle the explosive. Even in our time tyranny had
to give way in Germany, Italy, Greece, and poor down-
trodden Egypt. Russia cannot hold out for ever against
Nihilism ; and the Negro in the United States will not
continue to endure the wrongs which are being inflicted
upon his race until the end of time, any more than
other nations. Let experience speak, and the awful
dread of irreparable consequences have weight with
the Yankees. Every day the pressure grows, the fric-
tion between the two races gets more severe, and the
rising tide of education is making the Negro more
sensitive to his wrongs and the mockery of the words
of the constitution. If the government does not fall
back upon the law and maintain its dignity, if the
majority does not blend order with freedom and safety
with progress, the tide which is steadily rising will
crumble piecemeal the old cliffs of the constitution ;
and woe to them who live in a fool's paradise ! May
heaven forgive the folly of the strong and defend the
weak is the sincere wish of every Negro.

CHAPTER II

EARLY LIFE.

Life is like the transition from class to class in a school. The
schoolboy who has not learnt arithmetic in the early
classes cannot secure it when he comes to mechanics in
the higher: each section has its own sufficient work. He
may be a good philosopher or a good historian, but a bad
arithmetician he remains for life, for he cannot lay a
foundation at the moment when he must be building the
superstructure. The regiment which has not perfected
itself in its manœuvres on the parade ground cannot learn
them before the guns of the enemy. And just in the same
way a young person who has slept his youth away, and
become idle and selfish and hard, cannot make up for that
afterwards. He may do something: he may be religious
—yes; but he cannot be what he might have been. There
is a part of his heart which will remain uncultivated to
the end. The Apostles could share their Master's suffering—they could not save Him. Youth has its irreparable
past.

—F. W. ROBERTSON.

YES, "Youth has its irreparable past," but the misfortunes of youth were not self-imposed; it was the
tyranny of slavery which loaded Walter Hawkins, as
soon as he was born, with calamities, most of which
he has never been able to overcome. While some only
know misery by comparison with their own happiness,
this man was made to experience it before he could
understand what it meant. From his birth he was

(26)

made to go under a dark, bleak rock—on a sunless shore—in company with those who could not explain why he was born to such a cruel fate. They could not even pity him, since they themselves were martyrs to the same heartless destiny. Himself and they might have felt that there was a thing called happiness by people whom they had seen laughing, or singing those sacred songs which he would one day learn : that was the only cup of consolation they had to drink from. But as years rolled on, and the slave-driver compelled him to speak in subdued tones, it was then the child began to comprehend the mystery of the sunless path—which afterwards made him incapable of being in love with his fate. What he would have been if he had not been born, nursed, and spent his early days in bondage we cannot tell ; this we will venture to say from what we shall learn from his life —there was the making of a man worthy of any race in the slave child.

Bishop Walter Hawkins was born at Georgetown, Maryland, in the district of Columbia, in or about the year 1809, at a time when the United States no less than Great Britain were beginning to be stirred from centre to circumference with the anti-slavery agitation. His father and mother were both pure-blooded Negroes, whose ancestors were among the millions that were stolen from the bosom of their fatherland to supply the labour market of America. They were both slaves at the time of the birth of their son Walter. At the age of forty his father was encouraged by the Quakers

—whom we have said were the first to free their slaves in the United States—to work overtime after he had fulfilled his long day's work for his master. In this way the poor man managed to save the sum of 365 dollars (£73 4s. 2d.), with which he purchased his liberty. Heaven only knows what the slaves would have had to go through, but for the humanity and practical sympathy of those unostentatious Christians. Bishop Hawkins does not seem to remember much about his mother, for she died when he was quite young. Although the children lost much by her death, it certainly was great gain to this mother, who dared not call the children of her anguish her own. What a glorious emancipation was hers! Better far is thy lot to be numbered with the dead than to have lived to be hunted down by bloodhounds or whipped by ex-convicts. What a glorious transformation is thine! Thy death was a far better thing than the insults of bullies more degraded than thyself. Was thy death not preferred, than to live to see thy loved ones torn one by one from thy heart, and sent off in the chain-gang never to see them in the flesh any more, or, what is worse, to see and not to know that they were verily part and parcel of thyself?

Out of a large family, the Bishop can only remember two brothers and two sisters. Who knows but that before Walter was born the others were carried into the south, from whence it was believed that neither the living nor dead ever returned to relate the horrors of the life of a slave in yonder region? The eldest of

the two sisters died, while the eldest brother, determined no longer to serve his master, ran away; we
hope he was never recaptured. The Bishop, one
sister, and a younger brother—who fell down a flight
of stairs, in consequence of which he became a cripple
for the rest of his life—was all the family left to
Hawkins the elder. The cripple was given as a present to the old man, but he did not enjoy the present
of his own son for long, for he followed his mother
into the eternal world. Listen to the heartless language of this descendant of a convict : " Old man, you
can have him; he is of no use to me ". Nevertheless
the man was glad to have one free child, though he be
a cripple. At the death of the master the remaining
two children became the property of widow Jane
Robinson, the sister of one Robert Beverly, a rich
squire, who always supplied her with all the necessaries of life, as she was what they called very poor.
And a most eccentric creature was this Jane Robinson.
Following the custom and spirit of the age, she professed the popular religion. She used to teach young
Hawkins to lie on her behalf, but would have him
whipped if he did so on his own responsibility, or
threaten him with being " cast into a lake of fire and
brimstone "; not her religious belief, but the effect of
slavery on the slave-holder made them so inconsistent
as to say to the slave boy: " If there is a knock,
put on a clean white apron, and go to the door, open
it, and if it is Mrs. Thomas Bell or Mrs. Frank Keys
tell her I am gone out ". Evidently old Jane believed

that there must have been some virtue in a "clean
white apron"; perhaps it served to cover a multitude
of sins. Not content with putting this lie into the
boy's mouth, she would stand off where she could hear
him tell the lie, and having satisfied herself that the lad
had done his duty well, *i.e.*, according to her moral
standard, she would laugh with delight, like a daughter of an ex-convict, at the exploits of her illustrious
father's dashing acts of villainy. Having done this,
old Jane would say: "Go to your work (not with a
clean white apron) in ten minutes". When she
thought that he was there she would go and look
around and say, pushing the soil with her foot: "Are
you cutting the weeds all right, John?" If he replied
in the affirmative, when he was not strictly accurate,
old Jane Robinson would say, by way of exhortation:
"John, you must not lie. Don't you know that all
liars are cast into the lake that burns for ever?"
How was he to know? and if there were such a place
ought not old Jane to have the warmest corner? Who
is to be blamed if this boy grew up to be a hardened
liar? If it were just for him to lie for his mistress without fear of being "cast into the lake that burns for ever,"
why not do it for himself? Slavery was a bad—not
to say a hard—schoolmaster for the Negro; moreover
it was fruitful in respect of raising a race of men who
were at once semi-barbarous, immoral and degraded
physically as well as mentally. The Bishop says:
"Jane Robinson always had her prayers in her
private room three times a-day"; and he could often

hear her say : "O Lord, have mercy upon the poor
Africans!" and groaned as if her soul was really
troubled about them. But what avails prayers and
groans when she, like so many other slave-holders,
persisted in degrading the African? Yet these prayers
and groans constituted the religion of the pious Christians of Negro-driving America. Their ministers were
their paid puppets, who taught the slaves from the pulpit
that they must obey their masters and mistresses in
all things. These men of God did not think or feel that
it was beneath the dignity of their vocation to tell the
Negroes "that some He made masters and mistresses
for taking care of their children and others belonging
to them . . . others He hath made slaves and servants to assist and work for their masters and mistresses that provide for them, and some others He hath
made ministers and teachers to instruct the rest, to
show them what they ought to do, and put them in
mind of their several duties". God called them, but
the devil shook the bag.

The Right Rev. Bishop Meade of Virginia, in an
address to slaves, said : "Almighty God hath been
pleased to make you slaves here, and to give you nothing but labour and poverty in this world, which you
are obliged to submit to, as it is His will that it should
be so. Your bodies, you know, are not your own :
they are at the disposal of those you belong to." And
others of these paid "liars for God" published a cate-
chism for slaves, in which they had the impudence to
ask and answer the following questions : " Is it right

for a servant to run away, and is it right to harbour a
runaway?—No. What did the Apostle Paul do to
Onesimus, who was a runaway? Did he harbour him
or send him back to his master? Answer—He sent
him back to his master with a letter." Yes, and this
minister ought to have added: "Receive him not as a
servant but above a servant, a brother in Christ". Of
course the puppet was paid to keep the last clause
out—nay, more, the slave was even taught that "to
disobey his master was to yield to the temptation of the
devil". Bishop Hawkins tells us of one Parson
Baulch, who was accustomed to preach once a month
in the Presbyterian Church, in the neighbourhood in
which he lived, to the slaves. This venerable old man
used to take the same text, and preached the same
sermon for twenty years, as testified by his father and
grandfather, to which they were bound to listen, under
pains of being whipped. The text was: "Servants,
obey your masters," and the substance of the sermon
was: "Sam and Sukey, you must mind all you are
told to do by your masters, and obey. You must not
steal from them. Should they lose a pin, and you find
it, you must give it to them. You must not lie, and
you must not run away from them." While thus
speaking, he would put his finger on the supposed text
in the open Bible, and, looking in the gallery where
all the slaves were allowed to sit, would continue his
apology for a sermon by saying: "The Lord says (I
suppose the lord of mammon), if you are good to your
masters and mistresses, He has got a kitchen in

heaven, and you all will go there by-and-by ". What
if Parson Baulch is in that kitchen now? A more
hateful caricature of a sermon cannot be conceived
than this wretched mutilation of the righteous character of God. In every denomination were found men
of Parson Baulch's stamp, except the Quakers and a
few laymen who protested against this libel on the
Deity. But many of the slave-holders would carry it
away and repeat it (parrot-like) to the poor slaves.
Poor Jane Robinson had been pretty well off during
some portion of her husband's life, but, unfortunately
for her and her slaves, he ran through his money by
drinking and gambling, two offsprings of slavery, and
at last he died from the effects of his riotous living,
leaving old Jane, a son and a daughter in possession
of five slaves as their fortune, which was considered
very little to live upon ; consequently she became very
stingy in her fare. If she put herself upon a smaller
fare, it was certainly a bad look-out for the stomachs of
her five Negroes, who were soon after made to feel as if
their throats were cut. Inasmuch as her rich brother
Beverly came to her assistance and relieved her wants,
she continued to buy the cheapest meal and bread she
could find for her slaves. It was a part of the policy
of many of the slave-holders not to feed the Negro
too highly, and with that fear they gave him too little.
Just as they maintained that " if the slave were not
allowed to read the Bible " he would remain an intellectual infant, whom they could bend at will, but if
they were allowed to read it the game was up, so they

3

feared that by the perusal of such a book the slave
" would be converted not into a Christian, but a
demon," *i.e.*, he could no longer be kept in subjection.
Old Jane Robinson did with the food exactly what a
thousand masters and mistresses did with both food
and religion, viz., diluted and adulterated them in
quantity and quality to suit the peculiar institution in
which millions of human beings were kept as chattels.
The pinch of hunger made the young man yearn for
liberty.

Ye clouds ! that far above me float and pause,
Whose pathless march no mortal can control !
Ye ocean waves ! that, wheresoe'er ye roll,
Yield homage only to eternal laws !
Ye woods ! that listen to the night-bird's singing,
Midway the smooth and perilous slope reclined,
Save when your own imperious branches, swinging,
Have made a solemn music of the wind !
Where, like a man beloved of God,
Through glooms which never woodman trod,
How oft, pursuing fancies holy,
My moonlight way o'er flowering weeds I wound,
Inspired, beyond the guess of folly,
By each rude shape and wild, unconquerable sound !
Oh, ye loud waves ! and oh, ye forests high !
And oh, ye clouds that far above me soared !
Thou rising sun ! thou blue, rejoicing sky !
Yea, everything that is and will be free !—
Bear witness for me, wheresoe'er ye be,
With what deep virtue I have still adored
The spirit of divinest liberty !

—COLERIDGE.

CHAPTER III

LIFE AS A SLAVE.

The results of the institution of slavery was to encourage a
tyrannical and ferocious spirit in the masters—cast a
stigma upon free labour and at once degraded and de-
humanised the Negro. It is true that there were instances
of sympathy between some masters and slaves, but, unfortunately, it was more than outweighed by a long series
of the most atrocious acts of cruelty, which were practised
in their capture in Africa, on the voyages to America, and
on the plantations.

—S. J. CELESTINE EDWARDS.

On him alone was doom of pain
From the morning of his birth,
On him alone the curse of Cain
Fell like a flail on the garnered grain,
And struck him to the earth.

—ANON.

ALTHOUGH Spence deplored slavery as a lamentable
evil and regarded it as a great human wrong, and said
that it was a degradation to the blacks, an injury to
the master, and a detriment to society at large, yet
he tried to justify the system by saying that "the
Negroes had at all times abundant food; the sufferings
of fireless winter were unknown to them; medical
attendance was always at command; in old age there
was no fear of workhouse; their children were never
a burden or care; and their labour, though long, was
neither difficult nor unhealthy". Given that this is
absolutely true, we maintain that the system was

(35)

iniquitous, inasmuch as "it ignored the essential characteristic of the man—the existence". In the words of Sallust: "Of two natures, the one is common to us with the gods, the other with the beasts". Undoubtedly, slavery sought to obliterate the more vital, and verily denied the nobler, of these two natures. What is the use of an abundance of everything when one is deprived of his liberty? Nor is the crime of keeping a man a slave minimised by talking about "the amount of degradation resulting from any cause must be limited by the height from whence there was room to fall," for surely it is a come down for any man, however ignorant—though free—to be torn from his home by force and fraud, and transported like a convict into servitude for an indefinite period: a condition where every precaution was adopted to prevent intellectual improvement. Granted that the intellectual condition of the slave had not fallen from a height equal to that of the race in the home to which he was transported, was slavery calculated to raise him above the condition of his savage life? Mr. Spence answers: "Yes, a positive gain"; we say: "Prove your assertion". He answers: "Their conversation and domestic habits are cheerful, they are fond of singing and dancing of a very energetic description; visitors to the Southern States constantly express their surprise at the drollery and gaiety they meet with". A slave had no domestic life; singing and dancing were the opiates with which the poor wretches drowned their sorrows. It is a characteristic of the Negro to be—or rather to profess to be—as

happy as he can under the condition he is in, which
you, Mr. Spence, and too many others, mistook for
real contentment. In the happiest moment of their
life, there arose in some an irrepressible desire for freedom which no danger or power could restrain, no hardship deterred, and no bloodhound could alarm. This
desire haunted them night and day ; they talked about
it to each other in confidence ; they knew that the
system which bound them was as unjust as it was
cruel, and that they ought to strive, as a duty to themselves and their children, to escape from it, as the slaves
in Jamaica tried to do in 1732, unknown to them, and
later as their neighbours in St. Domingo succeeded in
doing : and such was the state of mind beneath all
their singing and dancing that, had they means as they
had desire, there would have been no slave-holder to
talk about the happiness of his slaves. To enslave men
successfully and safely it was necessary to keep their
minds occupied with thoughts and aspirations short of
the liberty of which they were deprived. Thus masters
gave the slaves some holidays, which served the
purpose of keeping their minds occupied with pro-
spective pleasures within the limits of slavery. It
was during these holidays that the young man could
go wooing ; the married man went to see his wife ; the
father and mother to see their children ; the industrious and money-making could earn a few dollars : it
was then that the strong tried their strength at wrest-
ling or boxing ; then the drinker drank plenty of
whisky, and the religious spent their time in praying,

preaching, singing and exhorting. Before these holidays their pleasures were in prospect, after they were pleasures of reflection; but for these holidays, which acted as safety-valves, the rigours of bondage would have been carried off by the explosive elements produced in the minds of the slaves by the injustice and fraud of slavery. In his savage state the Negro was at liberty to eat what he liked and could get by his own activity, but as a slave he was forced to have " Johnny cakes " and black treacle, with rare variation. This cake was made out of corn-meal, salt, and water, and baked on a piece of barrel-head. At dinner-time old Jane Robinson would call her slaves and give each of them a piece and a little molasses, which she would pour into a large plate so as to make it look much more than it really was; of course there was no blessing asked on this meal. The necessary preliminary having been gone through, Walter would receive his allowance with all the humility of one who had received a knighthood from his Queen. It is needless to say that he soon polished off the " Johnny cake," licked the treacle and bowed ready for more, to which Mrs. Robinson would gravely reply: "You young rascal, do you mean to breed a famine? Go to your work!" Can anyone wonder at slaves singing :—

> " We raise the wheat,
> They eat the corn ;
> We bake·the bread,
> They give us the crust ;
> We sift the meal,
> They give us the husk " ?

Of course, if the Negro asked for bread, the slave-holder was bound to give him a stone. Besides baking the corn-meal dough upon a piece of barrel-head, the slaves were accustomed to wash their hoes, put the dough upon it, and bake their cake before the fire; hence the name "hoe-cake". If the slave had not a variety of dishes he certainly had a variety of means of producing the same cake; thus, instead of cooking them on hoes and barrel-heads, they would roll the dough into a round lump and cover it with cabbage leaves, sweep away the ashes from the hearth, lay the dough upon the ground and cover it over with ashes and fire. Honourable exceptions there were, but they were few and hard to find, who did not try to get as much work as possible, at very little cost for food and clothing. Some masters and mistresses would send their slaves to the market to beg food, of whom Dame Robinson was one; and, when the slaves returned laden with provisions, they would take the food from them as if the provision was theirs and not the property of the slaves: a job Walter did not like, as the poor slaves often got more kicks than cabbages; so he used to turn round the first corner after he left his mistress's house and loaf about until he thought it was time to go home again, pulling a long face because people would not part with their sweet potatoes, etc., without money, which would force the old lady to go marketing herself, when Walter would follow her as light porter; but he seldom got any of the good things which he brought home for his mistress. The time came, however, when this young slave began to get tired of his way of spending an existence which seemed to have no end. Something whispered to him : "Muzzle not the ox that treadeth out the corn"; from whence the words came he knew not. As he could not read, he must have heard them from someone who could. However they came, he thought himself to be the ox, and that he was muzzled by slavery; so he made up his mind to take off his muzzle and go in for a good feed the first chance he got. But he remembered that the old parson had told them not to steal, lest they would be cast into a "lake which burned for ever," besides the lashing he would get. Hunger is a sharp thorn. If he ate anything which was not given to him, he would have been accused of theft. Supposing he risked the lash and the "burning lake," how was he to get at the old dame's store in which the food was kept? "Surely," thought he, " I work for what I get"; and, after all, what was the use of working and not getting enough food to satisfy his hunger? "It cannot therefore be wrong to take what I have worked for." Walter quieted his conscience by deciding to steal some food; so, whether it were stealing or not, he'd chance hell, the whip, and everything, and have a good round meal the first chance he had. They say everything comes to those that wait : so Walter waited for his opportunity; and one day, when Dame Robinson and her daughter went out, and knowing that she would leave the keys at home, Walter set his sister to watch while he hunted

everywhere he could think to find them; at last it
occurred to his mind to look under her pillow, and
there to his great joy he found them—a happy thought
for his hungry stomach. Having found them he made
for the store, where he took flour, lard, butter,
sugar, and as much of other good things as he could
find. With the flour and lard he made short cakes,
which he baked in a Dutch oven. When cooked, he
called his sister, and set himself to get "a good square
meal" for once in his life; and, having had enough, he
put away what he could not eat for another time.
Soon after they had finished, the old lady came home;
and, after having had her tea, she gave her slaves their
share; but Walter had had more than enough, consequently he hid the biscuits which she had given him
away. But the worst was to come. Thinking that
old Jane was taking her usual nap, one day, after this
event, Walter sat down in the garden munching away
at the sugar he had stolen; but the old dame, who
was evidently aware that she had been robbed, only
professed to have been asleep, and had slyly got up
and looked out of the window only to find the young
man eating her sugar. So she stealthily walked out
and sneaked beside him, as he sat by the side of
a large gooseberry tree eating gooseberries and sugar.
She exclaimed: "You young rascal, I have caught
you at last". You can imagine the young man's
surprise; he was like the boy who, being sent with his
father's dinner, sat down by the roadside, and was in
the act of eating it when his mother came upon him,

exclaiming: "Richard!" to which the boy coolly
answered: "Why, I did not expect you so soon".
But for his near-sightedness he would have seen his
mother coming. So also on account of Walter's
absent-mindedness he did not take precaution to eat
his sugar at night or when his mistress had gone out
again. But fate decreed otherwise. What could the
poor half-starved boy say? Yonder on the side of a
small hill stood some willow-trees; thither the old lady
proceeded, and reached up to break, from one of them,
a piece stout enough to wreak her old vengeance on the
thieving slave-boy. But good nature interposed, and
ere she attempted to break off the stick there came
a breeze which took her off her feet, by lifting the limb
of the willow as the branch ascended. She let it go,
and poor Jane Robinson fell and rolled down the hill-
side. Poor Jane! what if she were killed? That young
Negro would have been lynched in four quarters for a
crime he had never committed. Seeing the old dame
did not make any attempt to get up, Walter looked
down to see what had become of his mistress. What
thoughts must have rushed into Walter's mind!
Suppose she say he pushed her down or was directly
the cause of her falling? he dared not deny it;
whether he did or not, she would have been believed
if only she had made a charge, as there was no court of
appeal against the *ipse dixit* of a slave-holder. What
must he do? To run away and be recaptured would
make it appear as though he were guilty. But fear,
reason, compassion for the old dame moved the heart

of the Negro to go to her assistance and help the fallen.
While helping her up he thought: "I am doing this,
but I know she will hire a man who whips slaves to
whip me," feeling that she could not do it herself, as
he was bigger and stronger than he used to be. But
Jane Robinson was hurt, and the moment she got on
her feet she made for the house as quickly as possible,
to have the rest which she had disturbed to catch the
thief. Walter escaped his thrashing then only to
think it had to come, but night came and nothing was
said, and no Negro-whipper came; so the day's doings,
and the dread and horrors of the whip, were forgotten
in sleep.

Morning came, and the day passed without anything being said; finally, the culprit escaped his thrashing altogether. Why? Eternity alone will reveal,
for Walter has never been able to solve the problem.
All other attempts at whipping were held in reserve,
until he attended a midnight meeting and did not get
back in time to get his rest, so that he could not do
his work the next day with alacrity.

Thinking he had been carousing all night, she began
to pound him with the first thing she got hold of.
Poor fellow! he could do better with sleep than with
the stick; but what has that to do with the slave-
holder, who wanted work out of her slave?

The system under which he laboured forbade consideration and gave little practical sympathy to a
weary slave, and when it was time to rest, what had
the slave to sleep upon? The sleeping apartments,

if they could have been called such, had little regard
for decency. Old and young, male and female, married
and single, were glad to drop down like so many brute
beasts upon the common clay floor, each covered with
his or her own blanket, their only protection from cold
and exposure. How much of rest had a slave ? The
night, however short, was cut off at both ends : slaves
worked late and rose early. Then part of the night
was spent in mending their scanty clothing for
decency's sake, and in cooking their food for the
morrow—in fact, they were whipped for over-sleep
more than for drunkenness, a sin which the masters
rarely reproved ; while neither age nor sex found
favour for sleeping too much. If they slept too long
the overseer stood at the quarter door, armed like a
hedgehog, with stick and whip, ready to deal merci-
less blows upon those who were a little behind time.
Thus, when the horn blew, there was a general rush
for the door, each trying to be first, as the last one
was sure to get a blow from the brute. He was
accounted a good master who allowed his slaves to
leave the field to eat their hoe-cake and salt pork or
herrings ; those who had their meals in the field had
it thrown in a row in the corner of the fences or hedge,
so as not to lose time to and from the field.* Consequently loss of sleep was a great privation to the one
whose religious zeal had carried him to a camp meeting at night, for which he had to pay very dearly the

* *Life of Fred. Douglas.*

next day. Anyhow old Jane got square with Walter, for she paid him for his past offences. But hunger and thrashing had silently been doing their work in his mind. They served to create and intensify his desire to be free, which was brought to a climax one Sunday evening when old Jane began on his poor bones, which he could bear no longer, and he turned upon the old lady, looking fiercely at her. Being pressed with blows he raised his hand to strike her— what a damnable system that would prompt a man to strike a woman, however strong and wicked, much less old Jane Robinson!—but to his honour he did not let his hand come down upon her. The fierce look and raised hand cured her, for she never tried to whip him again, we hope, nor any of her other slaves.

It was nonsense for those who were free and lived by slavery to talk about the comfort of the Negro as a slave, when his monthly fare was eight pounds of pickled pork or its equivalent in fish ; the pork was often tainted and the fish was of an inferior kind. With his pork or fish he had given him one bushel of Indian meal, unbolted, of which fifteen per cent. was fitter for hogs than man ; with this one pint of salt was given. The yearly allowance of clothing was not more ample than the supply of food. It consisted of two tow-linen shirts, one pair of trousers of the same coarse material for summer, and a pair of woollen trousers and a woollen jacket for winter, with one pair of yarn stockings of the coarsest description. Children under ten years of age had neither stockings,

shoes, jackets nor trousers. They had two coarse tow-
linen shirts a-year, and when these were worn out
they went naked until the next allowance day.
Without the least regard to whether they were boys
or girls, men or women, beds they had none; one
coarse blanket was given them, *i.e.*, men and women;
the poor children had to huddle themselves where
they could in the corners of the huge chimneys, with
their feet in the ashes to keep them warm.*

Besides saying that the Negro was better off than
pitmen and sailors, Mr. Spence observed: " The mind
of the Negro avoids reflection on the past, and abstains
from investigating the future "; if they did not, they
ought to have been kept as slaves " for ever and ever ".
But slave-holders lived in a fools' paradise; what brute,
living in a climate such as Maryland, would not feel
the pinch of cold and hunger with the miserable fare
they were allowed? What man would not try and
kill, steal, lie, or do anything to satisfy these cravings?
Nay, how did these poor wretches survive under
that cruel curse? Why did they not rise and
mercilessly butcher the fiends who thus maltreated
them? Did they not know that " who would be
free, themselves must strike the blow"? Alas! Alas!
Starvation, cold and hunger conspired, and verily
took away what courage was left in them, when
they left the shore of their native land. Yet not all,
for there were slaves whose spirit no lash could ever

* *Vide Life and Time of Fred. Douglas,* p. 29.

conquer, whom labour, cold, hunger, and starvation could not make docile; these stole, escaped, killed bloodhounds, fought their overseers, and even died rather than be conquered—died martyrs for the liberty from which either they or their ancestors were stolen. Walter Hawkins shared this love of freedom and spirit of resistance to injustice. The close fist which only partly fed him on hoe-cakes and black treacle, the scanty clothing through which the fierce, cutting north-wester pierced and chilled his blood, the hard earth on which he slept, and the deprivation of calling himself his own, were the forces which made him reflect and haunted him like a nightmare, and made him think and lay his plans to be his own master.

What did the slave-holder know of the inmost workings of the mind of the Negro? Aboriginal barbarity and slavery were the only circumstances under which they had an opportunity of contemplating him. What use did they make of these opportunities to study them? None; and to this day the same ignorance influences the strong prejudices which abound in the United States against the Negro. He has characteristics of his own, as his white brethren have. There lies in him a simple-mindedness which is mistaken for a love of personal slavery. Indeed, he has little in his intellect that is separable from his warm affection; while men have deduced the absurd notion that the Negro is fit for nothing but subservience to the superior race, they forget that it took their race thousands of years to evolve a Darwin from the ape condition. Cicero thought that a Briton was unfit to serve the accomplished Atticus.

While smarting under this sense of the injustice of the institution of slavery, the son of Mrs. Robinson, who had followed his father's footsteps in drinking and gambling, came home one day hard up for cash, and, not knowing any better way to raise money to satisfy his passions, resolved on selling Walter, whom he called, saying : " Do you want a master ? " Of course, he had no other choice but to answer : " Yes, sir ". So he took the young man to a slave-dealer who bought and sold slaves to owners in the South. The dealer and southern plantations brought to his mind all the terrible things he had heard about those parts, and well he might, for the law by which slaves were governed in the Carolinas was a provincial law as old as 1740, but was made perpetual in 1783. By this law every Negro was presumed a slave unless the contrary appeared. In the ninth clause, two justices of the peace and three freeholders had power to put slaves to any manner of death. The evidence against them might have been without oath. No slave was to traffic on his own account. Any person who murdered a slave was to pay £100, or £14 if he cut out the tongue of a slave. Any white man meeting seven slaves together on a high road could give them twenty lashes each, and no man could teach a slave to write under a penalty of £100 currency. The terrors of the South had nothing to do with young Robinson, who wanted money, which he valued much more than a Negro. Walter stood by while the bargain was being made, and heard the dealer offer nine hundred dollars for his body. Speaking to Walter, he said : " Can you plough and grub ? Can you do general work on the farm ? " The poor fellow could do no more than please his master by answering " yes " to all his questions, which pleased both the dealer and young Robinson, for whose benefit all the lies were told. The bargain being struck, an arrangement was made for Walter to re-appear the next morning at seven o'clock; at the same time, he was to bid good-bye to his friends; but be sure, said he, that you are on the spot at seven. Knowing that he did not mean to go, though his master had had the price of his body in his pocket, the young man, who might have been weeping, put his thumbs under what ought to have been a vest, whistling " Hail, Columba ". Being tired of whistling, he began to think : " You will never see me again, old man ; what a fool you were to part with your money before you got your goods ". But Walter had not yet realised the difficulty of the situation. So complete were the ramifications of the slave system that a slave could not get away as easily as he imagined. Still resolved to flee, he went straight to his old father and told him that he was sold. " Sold !" exclaimed the old man ; " to whom ? " " Why, to old Cidley, the Negro-dealer." After a pause the old man said : "They will sell my last child," and burst into tears, weeping like a child. He talked and wept with his son until he bathed the floor at his feet. At last he said : " Boy,

4

run away". "I will," responded Walter. But now his troubles began, for he did not know, and the old man could not tell him, where to go any distance beyond ten miles in either direction from where they stood, as it was a part of the policy of slavery to keep them in ignorance as to distance. But if resolution could not break rocks, it could climb mountains. As night came on, the old man lay down to find consolation in sleep. Then it was that Walter crept out of the house into the open field, looking up to the stars, begging them to befriend a poor Negro in his endeavour to make good his escape from slavery. But, alas! there was no answer. Suddenly a thought struck him to go and see a young man whom he had met at a midnight meeting, and who was a Christian. He ran and walked until he arrived at the boarding-house in which he was employed as a waiter. He rapped at the door, and, as fate would have it, there was no one in but himself. Looking out of the window, he called out: "Who is there?" "It is I, Robert!" The young man opened the door and told Walter to come in. Then Walter told him all his troubles and his resolve. "Stop here," replied the sympathising fellow. But woe to Robert if they had caught him in his room! There Walter remained undisturbed for nearly four weeks.

Certainly when the next morning came there was no Walter to be found, and we can well imagine the kind of advertisements, placards, and bloodhounds that would be set on his track, besides the pressure that would be brought to bear on the old man, his father, to tell where his son was. Of course he could not tell, as he did not see him go away. And what were the thoughts of the runaway? Uppermost in his mind would be the fact that his father and sister would be wondering whether he was recaptured, famishing in the woods, dead, or being driven in a slave-gang, such as they had seen with dread passing through the town. We will give here an account of one of these gangs as witnessed in Virginia by an Englishman about seventy-five years ago. " I took the boat this morning and crossed the ferry over to Portsmouth, the small town which I told you is opposite to this place. It was a court day, and a large crowd of people were gathered about the door of the court-house. I had hardly got upon the steps to look in when my ears were assailed by the voice of singing, and, turning round to discover from what direction it came, I saw a group of about thirty Negroes of different sizes and ages following a rough-looking white man who sat carelessly lolling in his sulky. They had just turned round the corner, and were coming up the main street to pass by the spot where I stood, on their way out of town. As they came nearer, I saw some of them loaded with chains to prevent their escape, while others had hold of each other's hands, strongly grasped, as if to support themselves in their affliction. I particularly noticed a poor mother with an infant sucking at her breast as she walked along, while two small children had hold of her apron on either side, almost running to keep up with the rest. They came along singing a little wild hymn of sweet and mournful melody, flying, by a divine instinct of the heart, to the consolation of religion—the last refuge of the unhappy—to support them in their distress. The sulky now stopped before a tavern, a little distance from the court-house, and the driver got out . . . then he, having supplied himself with brandy, and his horse with water (the poor Negroes, of course, wanted nothing), stepped into his chair again, cracked his whip, and drove on, while the miserable exiles followed in funeral procession behind him."

> Over the spirits there came
> A feeling of wonder and sadness—
> Strange forebodings of ill,
> Unseen, and that cannot be compassed.
> As at the tramps of a horse's
> Hoof on the turf of the prairies,
> Far in advance are closed
> The leaves of the shrinking mimosa;
> So at the hoof-beats of fate,
> With sad forebodings of evil,
> Shrinks and closes the heart,
> Ere the stroke of doom has attained it.

Chapter IV.

ESCAPE FROM SLAVERY.

The desires of a people are seldom prejudicial to liberty, because
  they commonly spring from actual oppression or an apprehension of it.
    —Machiavelli.

Pursuing these ideas, I sat down close by my table, and, leaning
  my head upon my hand, I began to figure to myself the
  miseries of confinement. I was in a right frame for it,
  and so I gave full scope to my imagination.
    —Sterne.

No wonder that Sydney Smith said : " No virtuous
man ought to trust his character, or the character of
his children, to the demoralising effects produced by
commanding slaves. Justice, gentleness, pity and
humanity soon give way before them ; conscience sus-
pends its functions. The love of command, the maintenance of restraints, get the better of every other feeling, and cruelty has no other limit than fear." Think
what the feelings of this young Negro must have
been in his hiding-place, as all the horrors of a
slave-gang stared him in the face. Trembling, but
never dreading his danger, he crept out one night,
and hastened to tell his poor father and sister that
he was still on the best side of the chain-gang.
The moment he opened the door, his step-mother

(53)

told him to go out, for the hunters had been
there several times a-day with the bloodhounds to
hunt him down. The poor fellow begged to see his
father, but the woman, knowing and fearing the
penalty of his being seen there, insisted on his leaving
the house, and that right away; so he obeyed and
stepped out of the door. Just as he did so, one of the
two-legged bloodhounds who were looking for him entered the gate. While he hesitated to see whether
Walter was his prize, the lad bolted like a shot out of
a cannon. Kind fate had interposed, for the constable
had not his dogs with him that time, or he would have
captured his man. It was little use the fellow giving
chase to a young man running for his life and liberty,
for Walter soon left him out of sight and sound, and
back he went to his hiding-place at his friend Robert's,
where he arrived with the perspiration dripping from
his face, while his whole body was trembling with fear.
Robert not being in on his arrival, Walter sat down to
recover himself, and he no sooner gathered himself together than Robert walked in, and wanted to
know what was the matter. "Why," said Walter,
" I had a narrow escape of being caught by the constable." "Then," replied Robert, "you must go from
here now; you can't stay any longer"; for he knew
that if the two-legged bloodhound had kept up the
chase he would be sure to make enquiry there, and, if
found, he would be severely punished for harbouring a
runaway. " I can't," said Walter, " as I don't know
where to go, and I have no money to get food with."

The good friend put his hand in his pocket and took out
a five-dollar note, saying: "This will take you to a free
country". Then arose another difficulty, viz., the
passport, in the shape of free papers, that he might
show when he went for his railway ticket. So Walter
said: "I have no free papers, and I don't know any
way to get them. I have not even any white to be
my friend to say I am free." To be sure, no white
man in that part of the country would tell a lie or
disgrace himself by helping a Negro to make good his escape. So why dream about it? "Now is your chance
to make the best of a bad job," said Robert. While
they were thus discussing, another freed man came in,
not knowing that Walter had taken refuge there: so
that Walter had to tell him his troubles, and how he
had escaped the constable. "Why," said the fellow,
"the hounds have just gone by; 'tis a wonder they did
not stop here and ask or search for you. Here is five
dollars; it will take you where you want to go." Yet
neither he nor Robert could tell the runaway the exact
route he was to take. "Anyhow," said they, "go, and
we will pray for you if you will pray for yourself."
Blessed encouragement! Well might Tennyson make
Edith say :—

> "God help me! I know nothing—can but pray,
> For Harold pray—pray, pray, no help but prayer,
> A breath that fleets beyond this iron world
> And touches Him that made it."

Why should not these two Negroes pray for their
friend who was suffocating in bondage, and now seeks

to breathe fresh air ?   " What an asylum hath the
troubled soul in prayer." In the awful solitude of
night, in the yearnings of the soul for freedom from
physical or moral bondage, and in the thrill of sacred
emotions which stirs our inmost soul, there is consolation in prayer.   Now, if the slave-holder prays to God,
why should not the slave pray ?   Surely if the Deity
loves justice and abounds in compassion He might help
the poor Negro.

Robert discussed the route to the free country with
both his friends, and gave Walter what hints he could,
and bade the runaway " Godspeed ".

Having taken leave of Robert, Walter and his other
freed friend started and arrived at the house of the
latter in perfect safety.   Here he stayed from Friday
night until Monday morning.   When the day dawned,
and ere the monarch of the day began to scale the
horizon, Walter was up and made for the depôt (railway station), where he found crowds of people, both
white and black, taking their tickets for Baltimore—
the whites were being served first.   Our runaway stood
aside until everyone had been served, and then he
stepped boldly to the wicket door to get his, when he
was saluted by the ticket-seller with " Good-morning,"
quite a coincidence, as blacks were always expected to
salute first.   Having returned the compliment, he
asked for a ticket.   " Where are you going ? " was the
next query, asked in a short, sharp tone (as if to throw
him off his guard), although very good-naturedly.
" Baltimore," was the ready reply, with the compli-

mentary, "sir". According to custom he ought to have asked Hawkins for his papers, but the quick reply, spoken in a confidential tone, brought the ticket, and Walter handed him the money. The booking-clerk went on writing, and the other made his way to the railway carriage, took his seat in a dirty one, in which only Negroes were made to travel. Not many minutes after the train started off, having in the same compartment a few Negroes, but fearing lest they should speak to him, and therefore the more readily recognise that he was a runaway, or cross-question him in a manner that might lead him to betray himself, Hawkins played the fool by whittling some pieces of wood which he had picked up about the station, and, taking some strings out of his pockets, and a piece of paper, made and unmade a parcel until he arrived at Baltimore. Here he got out.

Being hungry, he asked a boy to show him a place where he could get some food, who directed him to a basement which was used as an eating-house. While going down the steps a fine-looking man met him face to face. "Good-morning," said he to Walter, with a knowing sort of look, which aroused the suspicion of the runaway. Keeping his wits about him, he continued down and asked the price of a meal, when he was told it would be twenty-five cents. In this place he happened to see his own likeness on a bill which he thought contained a reward for his capture. At once he thought that the man who had spoken to him was not his friend, but one who was looking out for runaways. So he put on a bold front, gave the man

twenty-five cents, and asked him to keep the food
warm for him. If the man is still keeping that eating-
house, he may be keeping the food warm yet, for, instead of returning, he took to his heels, leaving both
the food and the man behind him. When he got out
of sight he asked another boy—he was afraid to address an adult—to tell him the name of the nearest
free State, and where he could get a car that could
take him there. " Look ! " said the little fellow,
" there they are, and they will be going soon ! " We
ought to tell the reader that Baltimore was one of the
centres of the anti-slavery movement, and it was in
that city that Benjamin Lundy, the John the Baptist
of the new era, established an anti-slavery journal,
The Genius of Universal Emancipation, in 1821, and
laboured until 1831, at which time he wrote : " I have,
within the period above-named (ten years), sacrificed
thousands of dollars of my own earnings. I have
travelled upwards of five thousand miles on foot, and
more than twenty thousand miles in other ways ; have
visited nineteen States of this union, and held more
than two hundred public meetings ; have performed
two voyages to the West Indies, by which means
the emancipation of a considerable number of slaves
has been effected, and the way paved for the enfran-
chisement of many more." It was in this same city
that Dr. Buchanan delivered an oration in 1731 upon
the " Moral and Political Evil of Slavery ". What
would Walter Hawkins have given if he had only
known that there were such men at Baltimore as

Quaker Lundy? It was not to be, so he made his way
to the depôt; when he got there he found a crowd
similar to what he met at the first railway station.
Instead of waiting, as he had done before, he pressed
forward, only to be cursed and sworn at by the booking-clerk, to stand by while the white people got served;
but there was danger in that, as he might have been
seen by the man, who would certainly not lose sight
of him again. So with all the cheek imaginable he
pushed his way within the barrier. When the fellow
demanded to see his free papers, without any hesitation he pulled out the bundles which he had made of
whittled wood, etc., in the train on his way from
Haverdegrass to Baltimore. But by another happy
coincidence for him the ticket-seller did not ask him
to open it, but simply gave him a ticket. Without
further ceremony he made his way to the proverbial
black people's car, and soon the train steamed out.
No sooner had he made himself comfortable than they
crossed a river which made him think that he was
being taken back to Washington, but it was a false
alarm, because he was only crossing into the State of
Delaware, famous for being one of the first States
where the Quakers began to emancipate their slaves,
and about this time Delaware had only about three
thousand slaves. There they stopped, but Walter did
not get out, and happily no one came to look for him
while the train was in the station. Off she started
again, but it was a long time before the train stopped
again; whatever station this was he did not know nor

did he ask, for he was as much afraid to trust a Negro as a white man, nor would he get out to procure some food, as he had had enough experience at Baltimore, the shock of which he had not yet quite recovered from ; indeed, quietude and hunger were preferred to a full stomach and slavery, therefore he kept his seat, and made himself as happy as possible under the circumstances. At last the train ran into Wilmington: he did not offer to move for the next three-quarters of an hour, a terrible long time for him (minutes were as long as days to him) : it was as though someone was waiting to lay hold of him. "Oh, what must I do? Shall I enquire of someone when the train is going to start and where she is going?" Neither the grandeur of the city nor the beautiful scenery around had any charm for the runaway ; everyone who passed the railway carriage appeared to him like a ghost. While he was thus agitated a man entered the carriage in which he sat and began making signs and all sorts of unintelligible sounds, but neither the one nor the other could draw the badger. "You may shout, old fellow," thought he, "but you will have to talk before I get out of this car"; but the poor man was deaf and dumb, and what he wanted Walter does not know until this day. In the meantime the engine came up and hitched on to the carriage, but, just before starting, two Negresses stepped into the compartment in which he was sitting, for although they were well-dressed and nearly white they had to take their seat in the same filthy carriage in which the other

black people travelled, whether slaves or freed men.
The whistle blew and the train started; it was no
sooner out of the station than they sat one on either
side of Walter, the runaway, and addressed him with
a "good-afternoon," to which he replied: "Good-
afternoon, ladies, are you travelling any distance?"
"Yes," was the reply. My word, what a change had
come over him! How soon he broke the seal from his
lips! What a contrast between these and the other
people who had bidden him the time of day! "Are
you running away?" was the next poser they put to
him. "I have sold myself at last," thought he. If he
had kept up his reticence all might have been well, but
an answer was expected. "What shall I say? Shall
I tell a lie? Can I play the same trick as I played
upon the two booking-clerks I left behind me?"
These were the thoughts which rushed uppermost in
his mind. "If I tell a lie and escape, it will be better
than to tell the truth and be recaptured." So he
answered: "No, I am not". Of course, hesitation to
answer made the damsels ask more questions. "Have
you ever travelled any before?" which produced
further embarrassment. As he might as well be hung
for a sheep as a lamb, he answered: "Yes". Still
these ladies were not satisfied, so they had to further
cross-examine him. "Were are you going?" Having
overcome his difficulty, as he thought, he most readily
replied: "To Philadelphia". Still they pressed him
with another query: "Have you ever been there?"
Although he had not, he found no difficulty in saying

"Yes". But the ladies, who professed they were seeking for information, demanded of him to tell them what sort of a place the city of William Penn was. To which our friend confidentially replied : " Well, ladies, it is a fine place, filled with great big brick houses," at which they laughed heartily, for they belonged to the place. Knowing he was the man for whom they were looking, they replied : " We live in Philadelphia, and have seen the bills advertising for you, and we are sent by friends to find you before they take you back to the South. Are you hungry ? " Hunger was not the name to express his condition, for he could have eaten a donkey and given chase to the rider. The news sounded too good to be true ; nevertheless he answered : " Yes ". Then they opened one of their baskets which contained all sorts of dainties, and told him to help himself, which he most assuredly did, for he ate and ate until he felt uncomfortable about the buttons. After a chat poor Walter Hawkins fell asleep, a thing he would not have done if he had had no confidence in the integrity of the ladies. He slept the rest of the journey, and never woke until one of them said : " We are in Philadelphia ". The poor fellow awoke to find that he had been resting his weary head upon the lap of one of these angels of peace. On opening his eyes he caught sight of the lovely black eyes of the damsel looking at him with so much sweetness and compassion that, to use his own words : " I did not want to get up "; moreover, it was the most comfortable pillow he ever had in his life. When he got up she said : " You are free now "—a statement which he could not believe though he had undergone so much trouble to obtain it, but his friends reassured him that he was really free ; and, having given him some instructions about his movements in the city, they got out of the carriage while he stood overwhelmed with astonishment. At last the ladies bade him farewell.

Philadelphia has the honour of being the city in which the convention to frame the Federal Constitution met on the 25th of May, 1787, when the illustrious George Washington was chosen president, and it was there, on the 8th of August of the same year, that Governor Morris of Pennsylvania made his famous speech, which ran as follows : " I never would concur in upholding domestic slavery. It was a nefarious institution. It was the curse of heaven on the States where it prevailed. Compare the free regions of the middle States, where a rich and noble cultivation marks the prosperity and happiness of the people, with the misery and poverty which overspreads the barren wastes of Virginia, Maryland, and the other slave States. Travel through the whole continent and you will see the prospect continually varying with the appearance and disappearance of slavery. The moment you leave the Eastern States and enter New York the effects of the institution become visible. Passing to the Jerseys and entering Pennsylvania every criterion of superior improvement witnesses the change. Proceed southwardly, and every step you take through the great regions of slavery present a desert, increasing with the increasing proportion of this wretchedness. Upon what principle is it that the slaves shall be computed in the representation? Are they men? Then make them citizens and let them vote. Are they property? Why, there is no other property included! It comes to this, that the inhabitants of Georgia and South Carolina who go to the coast of Africa, in defiance of the most sacred laws of humanity, tear away their fellow-creatures from their dearest connections and damn them to the most cruel bondage." This powerful speech was followed by others, but we have not room to quote them. In 1794 we find that an anti-slavery convention was held in Philadelphia, in which nearly all the Abolition Societies of the States were represented, and at which a memorial was drawn up and addressed to Congress, praying it to do what it could to suppress the slave traffic. In 1795 another meeting was held in the city, when the Act of Congress was read: "An act to prohibit the carrying out of the slave trade from the United States to any foreign place or country". And, finally, it was in the city of Philadelphia that certain Negro citizens met in 1800 and drew up and presented a memorial to Congress calling attention to the slave trade between the United States and the coast of Guinea.

Chapter V.

"FOUND AT LAST."

Disguise thyself as thou wilt, slavery! Still thou art a bitter
draught; and though thousands, in all ages, have been
made to drink of thee, thou art no less bitter on that
account. Is it thou, liberty? Thrice sweet and gracious
goddess! whom all, in public or in private, worship; whose
taste is grateful, and ever will be so, till nature herself
can change.

—STERNE.

AT the time when Walter Hawkins arrived in Philadelphia it was called a free city and county; yet the young
ladies, who gave him the information that he was free,
dared not be seen with him after they had left the train,
so that he had to do the best he could. He was told that
there were always kidnappers hanging about on the
look-out for runaway slaves, through whom he might
be taken back to the dark South. While groping
about the city, he met a lad whom he thought he
could trust, and asked him if he knew the where-
abouts of one Walter Proctor. "Yes!" said the lad.
"Show me where he lives," said the runaway, "and
I'll pay you"—not that he had more money than wit.
With that offer the little fellow willingly led him
quite a distance from where he was standing towards
the abode of Uncle Proctor. At last his guide said:

5 (65)

" Look down there in that cellar! " But the man whom he had been seeking heard them talking, and, looking up, threw down his work, he being a shoe-maker, and ran up the steps, singing: " God *will* answer prayer, God *will* answer prayer! " With that hymn in his mouth he seized Walter, the runaway, by the arms, and took him down into the cellar, saying: " I knew that God would answer prayer ". To his unutterable joy, the old man said : " Boy, where have you come from? " " Home, sir," he replied. " Well, well; your eldest brother lives here, in this city, and has been here for years, and both of us have been praying for you." This old Negro was a Methodist minister to his race in the city, and was highly esteemed by all who knew him. The Bishop says : " He was a good man, one who exhibited in his daily life and conversation a sanctity which showed he lived in a city whose builder and maker is God ". Blessed saint ! the Eternal, not ourselves, will reward thee for thy goodness and humanity to many of thy oppressed race, above and beyond all thy expectation. We have not seen thee, nor have had the privilege of being blessed by thy hospitality, but thou hast given to one of our down-trodden race such of thy bounty as thou couldst. God blessed thee and thine. Farewell ! The dear old man took Walter to his brother's house. When he arrived there, he was disappointed to find that he was not at home ; but his good wife took him in, though she had never seen him before. There he sat in another room alone until his brother returned from his work, at a boarding-house where he was employed. When he came and entered the room in which his younger brother was sitting, they were both speechless, as they looked at each other. Hawkins the elder walked out, went upstairs whistling and came down again, into the yard and back again to the room. Why this strange conduct? Surely he must know his brother! But he did not; until the younger brother laughed and stood up. The poor fellow stepped up to him, and they both embraced each other, and remained silent for about ten minutes, being lost in rapturous ecstasy, neither knowing what the other had said.

At last Hawkins the elder broke the spell with: "I have been praying for you to be free. Where did you come from, and how?"

Of course, Walter had to tell his whole story through. His hairbreadth escape from the slave-gang, how he dodged the constable at his father's gate, after nigh a month's hiding in his friend Robert's room; how the latter and his friend gave him ten dollars, with which he got his railway ticket; how he played the fool in the train on his journey to Baltimore, and the narrow escape he had while going down a basement to get some food, and all about the pretty young ladies who befriended him in the train from Wilmington to Philadelphia.

But how did the runaway know there was ever such a man in Philadelphia as Walter Proctor the good? When he was a slave at old Jane Robinson's—beside Parson Baulch, who used to preach roaring sermons to the slaves—once a month special preachers visited the neighbourhood to conduct services such as Moody and Sankey did in England. These special preachers very frequently were black freed men, who had permission from the local mayor to hold forth for nine days only ; so it happened that old Proctor had visited his town a few times. Hawkins took these opportunities to have some personal interviews with the old man, by which means he got to know that, once he reached Philadelphia, he would be in a free city. Now, these itinerant Negro preachers were not permitted to remain in a slave district any longer than the specified nine days, and if they stayed longer they were at once put under arrest, as rogues and vagabonds, and lodged in gaol. After a time they were sold (if no one came to pay their fine) to the highest bidder, for the gaol fees, etc. The buyer would then hold them in bondage as long as he desired, for the money he had paid ; or—if he saw a chance of turning over an almighty dollar—sell them to another, worse or better than himself.

These preachers knew what it was to confront night, storms, hunger, accident, ridicule, and all manner of rebuffs, in order to carry some consolation to the poor slaves. It was this cup of consolation which gave the slave, who was not a drunkard, strength to bear his bondage with so much patience and toleration.

Although slaves were religious, the religion was neither deep nor sound. The religious instruction which they received did not represent the best view of Christianity. How could it, when the influence of the church was exerted continually to repress and to produce absolute outward submission ?

Such influence, even if it had been wholesome, could and did not penetrate deep or mould with much force the inner workings of the soul. It served to produce an outward conformity to the views of the master, while it left the heart of the slave untouched. Thus their religion as a whole was emotionalism, which found an outlet in those songs which rent the hills and filled the valleys at camp meetings with gladsome joy, and which made their taskmasters think that they had no longings for freedom.

How, then, could these people improve morally under conditions which violated every principle of the moral law ? It is said that paganism has no rule of right and wrong, no supreme and immutable judge, no intelligible revelation, and no fixed dogma; yet the paganism from whence the slaves were stolen was a better condition than the miserable caricature of Christianity in the midst of which they lived. The being of God, the facts of revelation, the universal brotherhood of man—whether he be evolved from apes or descended from the gods—the obligation of the moral law and immortality, were doctrines which masters believed concerned themselves; but they lacked charity to include the Negroes, for whom religion only served as an opiate to their cruel torture. Nevertheless, amid all the disadvantages of the iniquitous institution of slavery, and in spite of every prohibition to keep the light from the Negro slaves, a ray of light shone, thrown from the cross of Christ, into the souls of some few, through the preaching of fragments of the Gospel, which opened up a new world to them, whence they saw that through suffering and affliction there was a path which no slavery could block—a light which brightened the darkness of the present and reflected a halo of glory over the future, and gave their rude songs a ring of heartiness and certainty which electrified Jefferson and his countrymen so that they "trembled for their country". Their rude conception of religion gave the slaves a new language, which found expression in rapturous music : often labouring and suffering all day and singing all night sacred songs which in rude but impressive utterance set forth their sad fortunes and their hopes for the future. Where, in the whole annals of history, has there been found such a mighty chorus of music from bondsmen? The Jews wept by the rivers of Babylon, and the American Indians died under their yoke, but not so the Negro, who mocked his woes and chased his weary hours with some of the most thrilling music that ever fell on the ears of mortals. That such people should be kept in bondage for ever—or, now they are free, to re-enslave them—is impossible. While slave-owners thought that nothing would prevent them from keeping their slaves as such, the slaves realised an affinity—a mysterious relationship—between their spirit and the Spirit of the Universe, who would deliver them. It was in the profound belief in a Moral Governor of the Universe that the Negro centred all his hopes, all his latent perfections, and all his ideals of the future. In spite of all appearances to the contrary, they believed that the Supreme Will was good to each one of the beings whom it summoned and drew to itself.

In spite of all his errors, his failures, his corruptions, his miseries and environments, the Negro was never wrong in following the sacred impulse that impelled him to trust the invisible incentive, which ultimately raised him from the mire of social, mental, moral and religious degradation, in which slavery had placed him, to have confidence in God. "There are two ways," says Dr. Wescott, "by which we can attain the highest spiritual truth: the way of feeling and the way of thought." The Negro only knew the way of feeling, and this he used with all his might. Better it is to have all feeling and no thought than to have thought without feeling.

Law, whether written or unwritten, regulated the conduct of slaves. Masters knew that slavery was an institution inflicted upon an unwilling people. Thus, if they were out after prohibited hours, they were pursued by a posse of watchmen, and, if caught (or any one out of a number), they were lodged in gaol or the watch-house until the following morning, when they were taken out and whipped—the same principle was applied to both freed men and slaves. Nevertheless, if the slave had an indulgent master he would not let his slave be

whipped at the public whipping-post, but the poor
freed man could not escape.   It must not, however, be
supposed that the slaves always took the whipping
quietly, and endured every insult without a murmur,
for there were men like Frederick Douglas, who dared
to tackle a monster like Covey, while he fairly sickened
Hughes with a blow, and Knowls's Jim, who became
obdurate to the ill-treatment of slavery until he was
feared by constables, night watchmen, and even his
master.   This Knowls's Jim was the slave of a carriage-
builder whose name was Knowls; a Negro worthy of
his race.   He stood six feet two inches, well built
and as black as night.   The fellow had been ill-treated
once too often, and became indifferent, and finally only
worked when he got good and ready.   He was a good
workman, but when he would not work his master
was put to great inconvenience.   He managed to com-
pel respect by sheer force of character; yes, and he
loved his master! but one day a gang of slaves passed
through the town (similar to the one above described)
where they lived, and his master, who had the absolute right of disposing his property at will, sold Jim's
sister, who was also a slave, in his absence, not
thinking that anyone would dare to question his right.
However, on his return, Jim for some reason or other
asked for his sister—not dreaming that she had been
sold—when he was informed that Master Knowls had
sold her that day.   " Where is he ? " cried mad Jim—
for mad he was, the very thought of the poor girl being
loaded with chains, without bidding her good-bye, with

all the horrors of the gang and the dismal South, were
quite enough to transform a lamb into a lion, much
less the obdurate Jim. " Where is he ? " " I don't
know," was his mistress's reply. " By heavens ! " said
Knowls's Jim, " my sister shall come back, or I'll have
his life." The fellow rushed into the house, armed
himself with his pistol—for he owned one long before
this—and out he came. " The moment he comes I'll
shoot him, if I die the next moment." Well done,
brave fellow! "blood is thicker than water, and love is
stronger than death ". A million resolute Negroes like
Knowls's Jim would have settled the slave question in
America long before the Civil War. Nothing that they
could say to the big black Negro would satisfy him :
either his sister's deliverance from the brutal gang, or
two would die—the master by the hand of his slave,
and Knowls's Jim by the slave laws, which forbade a
Negro to touch a white man. Slave-holder Knowls was
neither without good sense nor feeling, therefore he sent
post haste after the captive maid, and bought her for
more than he had received for her. Brave son of Ham !
" If a man shall and must be valiant, he must march and
quit himself like a man, trusting imperturbably in the
Upper Powers, and, on the whole, not fear at all.
Now and always the completeness of his victory over
fear will determine how much of a man he is." Thee,
Knowls's Jim, we did not know personally, but have
learnt from thy love and courage to undeceive men,
that they might know that the love of kin and country
which has immortalised Greeks and Romans will yet

prove the saviour of our race. May thy children's children inherit thy unconquerable valour! Those who never held men as slaves, but had sympathy with the system, will regard such an act as Jim's with disfavour, and will probably censure his conduct as having been wicked on his part! But we who are descendants of slaves, or have been such, can offer no apology, because we know only too well that it was in the interest of the institution that we and our ancestors were watched and cowed. The masters had to deal with thinking animals like themselves, and not with wood, earth, and stone, and for their own safety and prosperity they had need to study, not so much the comfort of those animals, but the workings of the mind. They knew that slaves had little respect for a coward, and they felt the same contempt for a snarling slave. The operation of their minds they watched with practised skill: they learnt to read with trained eyes the state of their slave's heart and mind through their sable faces. Unusual sobriety, apparent abstraction, sullenness or indifference often afforded ground for suspicion and enquiry; not unfrequently an innocent man or woman was punished into confession of guilt they had never dreamt. Like the Inquisition, it was under such suspicion that a master would say: " You have got the devil in you, and I'll whip him out of you ". When it would have been more accurate to say that he, not the slave, was possessed by his Satanic Majesty. Suspicion and torture, being the instruments which they used to get at the truth, had the useful effect of either forcing them to run away like Walter Hawkins, or becoming callous like Knowls's Jim ; but more often it made these poor wretches appear joyous and content when they were suffering most intensely. In fact, these worse than wretched taskmasters had the saying: " When the nigger is down keep him down, for when the nigger rises hell rises "; and yet another of their inhuman sayings : " Give the nigger an inch, he'll take an ell; if you give the nigger a horse he'll drive it to hell ". No men, not even Spanish Inquisition-mongers, could have been more suspicious than slave-holders; and had Knowls's Jim killed his master, and himself lynched, we would have canonised him as a blessed martyr ere this. In these days, when we hear so much about the Negro problem in America and in the West Indies, we would tell alarmists that they need not worry themselves. The Negro requires neither pity nor patronage, but justice; and justice he will have, in spite of the hateful prejudices which withhold it from him, for the fate which determined his emancipation is determining his destiny in the near future.

CHAPTER VI

IN PHILADELPHIA.

A man who can give up dreaming and go to his daily realities;
  who can smother down his heart, its love or woe, and
  take to hard work of his hand; who defies fate, and, if
  he must die, dies fighting to the last,—that man is life's
  best hero.

—ANON.

THE ground on which the magnificent city is built was
purchased by William Penn, in January, 1683, from
some Swedish settlers. The site was chosen because
it stands on a neck of land between the Schuylkill and
Delaware rivers. Such is the natural beauty of the
position that its illustrious founder said, when he
selected the site of the city, it is " not surpassed by
any among all the places he had seen in the world".
He was drawn to the spot by the firmness of the land
and the pure springs and salubrious air, which Penn
regarded as a fit place for a city of refuge, a mansion
of freedom, and a home of humanity. While his
calm imagination surveyed his past success, the glory
of the future destiny of Philadelphia caused "pleasant
visions of innocence and happiness to float before the
minds of the Quaker brethren". " Here," they said,
"we may worship God according to the dictates of the
divine principle, free from mouldy errors of tradition;

(76)

here we thrive in peace and retirement, in the lap of unadulterated nature ; here we may improve an innocent course of life on a virgin elysian shore." There never was a city which had a more glorious origin than this, and few, if any, has had such success. The highest hope of the pure, humble-minded Friends were eclipsed when Philadelphia became the birthplace of Independence and the pledge of the Union. In March, 1683, the boundaries of the infant city were marked off. Streets of chestnut, ash, and walnut were laid out with trees of the original forest. Soon after it could boast of a few mansions, and became the scene of the legislation assembly. Each of the six counties into which Penn's dominions were divided elected nine representatives—consisting of English, Scotch, and Irish, as also Swedes and Dutch—for the purpose of establishing a charter of liberties. When the representatives of the democracy were assembled Penn, after having referred to the Government of England, said, concerning the laws of his dominions: "You may amend, alter, or add. I am ready to settle such foundations as may be for your happiness." To the people he said : "I am not like a selfish man ; through my travail and pains the province came ; it is now in Friends' hands. Our faith is for one another, that God will be our counsellor for ever." What could mortal say or do more? and how could the people and their representatives receive their charter otherwise than with unspeakable gratitude? Then one of the representatives, speaking for the others, said: "Of more than expected liberty". Penn replied, with his usual enthusiasm : "I desired to make men as free and as happy as they can be". What king, except a Quaker, would offer such liberty to his subjects? In the adjoining county, Maryland, the council were the puppets of Lord Baltimore, while in Pennsylvania they were named by the people. In Maryland, from the chief magistrate down to the most subordinate executive officer, the right of appointment rested solely with the proprietary, whereas in Pennsylvania every executive officer, except the chief, was elected by the people or their representatives, and the governor could peform no public act but by the consent of the council. "Lord Baltimore had a revenue derived from the export of tobacco, the staple of Maryland, and yet the colony was burdened with debt and taxes." When a similar revenue was offered to Quaker Penn he declined, and tax-gatherers were unknown in his province at the same time. In his old age the Quaker king wrote : "If, in the relation between us, the people want of me anything that would make them happier, I shall readily grant it". No wonder, when the semi-barbaric Peter, the Russian reformer, attended one of the Quakers' meetings in London, he exclaimed : "How happy must be a community instituted on their principles!" A hundred years later we find the philosophical Frederick of Prussia saying, after he had read the account of the Government of Pennsylvania : "Beautiful! it is perfect, if it can endure". Two

years after the foundation of the city of Philadelphia
it contained six hundred houses, with schools and the
printing-press in full swing. When it was three years
of age, this city had increased at a rate greater than
New York had done in the first fifty years of its existence. Such was its glorious prosperity that Penn
said : " I, without vanity, say I have led the greatest
colony in America that any man did upon a private
credit ; and the most prosperous beginnings that ever
were in it are to be found among us ". Yea, he might
have added : " Not only in America, but in the whole
world ". For neither of the great cities of antiquity
had such a lawgiver and guide as William Penn. It
was not until the government had been organised,
peace with the Indians had been confirmed, the
fundamental law established, and the courts of justice
instituted, that the uncrowned king felt that his mission had been accomplished. " Servant of God, well
done ! " There is nothing in the history of the human
race like the confidence which the simple virtues and
examples of William Penn inspired. What justness !
what liberality ! what judgment ! and what an incentive to the practice of virtues was his unselfish life !
Where shall we look for another like this Quaker
king ?—a preacher of righteousness, a peaceful warrior
—a statesman whom any age or nation would be
proud of. " A turbulent woman was brought to trial
as a witch ; Penn presided, and the jury consisted of
Swedes and Quakers. The grounds of the accusation
were canvassed ; the witnesses were calmly examined ;

and the jury, having listened to the governor's charge, returned this verdict: 'The prisoner is guilty of the common fame of being a witch, but not guilty as she stands indicted'. In what country in Europe at that age would the wretched woman have had the opportunity of giving bonds to keep the peace?" Not one.

When Penn had finished his great work in the New World he bade Philadelphia farewell—a happy farewell—in these touching words: "And thou, Philadelphia, the virgin settlement of this province, my soul prays to God for thee, that thou mayest stand in the day of trial, and may thy children be blessed". With these parting words—this benediction—he sailed for England, leaving freedom to its own development. We think we can hear the old sovereign saying, as he sailed down the Delaware: "My love and my life are with you, and to you; no water can quench it, nor distance bring it to an end". What would not this Quaker have done for the slaves who fled to his city for their freedom, if he had lived on? There never was such a man since the humane Solon! Oh, that the spirit of William Penn could but influence the corruption of the Republic which he helped to build!

About the time when the runaway slave Hawkins arrived in Philadelphia there were 18,708 Negroes living in the city, 250 of whom had paid for their freedom. Some were free-born, while others were—like young Hawkins—escaped slaves. These Negroes were not all paupers, living upon the charity of the bene-

volent white citizens ; because their real personal property was then valued at about 1,500,000 dollars. One
can well imagine the feelings of this young man, who
had never seen such a large number of his race con-
gregated into one town or city as freed men. However, the old preacher Proctor, in whose house he
found a refuge, and who introduced him to his elder
brother, kept him for a few weeks, feeding both his
mind and body. Such was the old man's intense love
to Christ and devotion to charitable works that, who-
ever came in his company, was made to feel a like
affection for One whom the ages have been slow to
comprehend. Before the end of the second week
Hawkins felt that old Proctor's influence was irresistible ; at last, while listening to one of his sermons, the young man became penitent, and threw in
his lot with the Christians, and resolved that "this
people shall be my people, and their God shall be my
God ". As a slave, his religion was mere emotionalism,
which served to break the monotony of the cruel
scourge of slavery. But as a freed man he had an opportunity of reflecting upon the character of Christ,
which had been clouded by the moral degradation
which pervaded all rank of the society from whence he
had made his escape. In that society vice reigned, yet
it was believed to be under the special protection of
Christianity—we mean the vice of breeding slaves and
encouraging drunkenness and the like. What a revolution must have been wrought in the mind of this
young man ! What else could have done it in the

6

short space of a fortnight, save beholding the spotlessness of Christ? The slave awoke in a new creation, with a new incentive to the practice of virtue, new motives for action, and new resolutions. Now he saw how Parson Baulch had misrepresented the religion of Christ; and how the hell and damnation exhortations were used as instruments to keep his mind and body in subjection to slavery. It was worth all he had undergone to get a truer portraiture of Christ—the Lord Paramount of Christianity. Whereas dear old Proctor attended mainly to his spiritual necessities; his own brother, and a number of friends, took delight in helping him physically. Some made clothes, and others gave him cents in order that he might go farther north, as Philadelphia was by no means the place that Penn designed it to be at this time. For, though it was called a free city, kidnappers were ever on the alert to recapture slaves who had taken refuge in it, and send them south again. Walter was told that the "spirits" were on his track, bills were posted everywhere, and that reward was offered for his body. Now, this anxiety to recapture a runaway slave was not so much for his value, as to deter others from running away. It was a vital part of the hideous system, to use every means and meanness to terrify. So he made up his mind to go far enough north to entertain no fear of being sent back to Cidly, who had paid for him. Hence he had to keep indoors for the most part, and never walked from old Proctor's to his brother's house at night alone. In short, he had to enjoy liberty under difficulty. To run away from slavery was a crime, consequently there was a sort of extradition treaty existing between the free and slave States, which said to slave-holders : " Prove your property wherever you find it, and take it home "; therefore, in time the Negro learnt that the safest place for fugitives was Canada or the islands of the sea. The latter he could not walk to, whereas he could tramp to the former, so Hawkins made up his mind to face all the difficulties which were before him, and make quite sure that he was really free. But he could not leave Philadelphia quite as William Penn had done, *i.e.*, with a benediction, but he could thank God for directing his steps thither, and for the hospitality which he had found in the city which gave independence to the United States. The little time he spent in it was such, however, that it refreshed him for his long journey. To leave old Proctor, who was more than kind to him, his brother, whom he had not seen since he was a child, and the many acquaintances he had formed, stirred his very soul; yet go he must. Liberty is too precious a jewel to be lost, and chance is a very uncertain game to play at, and the chances were if he stopped there he was almost sure to be recaptured. How different would have been the case if he had been in a Mohammedan's country! The great prophet did not abolish slavery altogether, for in that condition of society it would have been neither possible nor desirable to do so. He not only encouraged the emancipation of slaves, but " laid

down the principle that the captive who embraced
Islam should be *ipso facto* free, and he took care that
no stigma should be attached to the emancipated
slave in consequence of his honest and honourable life
of labour " * as a freed man.   Not so was the species of
Christianity which prevailed in America ; though the
slave became an angel he was treated, pursued, and
dogged as a slave ; in fact, the system was even worse
than Roman slavery, because the Roman slave-holder
made no profession of Christianity, whereas most of
the Yankee slave-holders did, and thereby caused the
name of God to be blasphemed to this day.   One cannot think how the Negro suffered prostration and
anguish of spirit, and yet evinced such a cheerful disposition and a light heart for three hundred years,
without rising in his wrath and cutting the throat of
the tyrant who kept him a slave.   Did he not feel
enough for himself and his race ? or was it the inherent
docility of his nature which enabled him to maintain
a dignified silence even when an effort of self-vindica-
tion might have led to his emancipation ?   Yes, it was
partly this, and the fact that the slaves had much
more of the spirit of Christ than their cruel masters.
Well did a writer in the *Westminster Review* of January, 1853, say : " Were we forced at this moment to
search for the saints of America, we should not be
surprised to find them among the despised bondsmen ".
Imperfect as was their knowledge of matters theological, they had more of the real spirit of Christianity

* *Mohammed and the Mohammedans.*

than the bondholders, in whom justice, gentleness, pity and humility had given way to barbaric actions, which counterbalanced all the evils of the excisemen, licensers and tax-gatherers of England in the dark ages. Most of the ministers of religion were as dead, spiritually, as their slave-holding paymasters. The love of command, the impatience of restraint, got the better of every other feeling; hence no character, however unblemished ; no respectability, however unquestionable ; no man, however holy, who was cursed with a hundredth portion of the blood of his Negro ancestors, escaped the stigma of the institution of slavery.

CHAPTER VII.

ON THE ROAD.

Write your name in kindness, love and mercy on the hearts of
thousands you come in contact with year by year; you
will never be forgotten. No; your name, your deeds, will
be as legible on the hearts you leave behind as the stars
on the brow of the evening.

—DR. CHALMERS.

THE friends in Philadelphia having made up a parcel
of clothes and collected some money, the fugitive now
got ready for his northward journey. From Philadelphia he crossed over into New Jersey. Although
the colony had not the glorious history of the one he
had just left, yet it could boast of an act, which was
passed as early as 1694, which provided, among other
things, for the trial of Negroes and other slaves for
felonies punishable with death, by a jury of twelve
persons, before three justices of the peace; for theft
before two justices, the punishment, if found guilty,
being whipping. Unfortunately for the Negro, this
law was afterwards supplanted by severe prohibitions,
requirements and penalties. The whites interpreted
"trial by jury" to mean one Negro's testimony to be
good against another in a trial for felony, and the right
of an owner to select his own jury. Humane masters

(86)

were denied the right of emancipating their own slaves.
A slave was prohibited from owning real property. In
1713 they enacted that a Negro belonging to another
province not having licence was "to be whipped and
committed to gaol; and people were punished for con-
cealing, harbouring or entertaining slaves of others ".
In 1714 the whites of New Jersey stripped the Negro
of every right he possessed a hundred years before, and
the general court ruled the man to be mere chattels
by levying an import tax of ten pounds upon every
Negro imported into the colony. In 1760 they put the
last straw on the camel's back by pushing him out of
the militia. Nevertheless, New Jersey became afterwards one of the great centres of the anti-slavery
movement, and was one of the first States in which
the Quakers emancipated their slaves (1780).* On the
24th of January, 1820, New Jersey passed six perti-
nent resolutions, a copy of which they sent to the
governor, whom they requested to forward to each of
the senators and representatives of this State in the
Congress of the United States against the extension
of slavery. Whereas the slave population of New
Jersey was 2254 in 1830, the number was reduced to
674 ten years after, *i.e.*, in 1840. Of course, Hawkins
felt no safer in New Jersey than when he was in
Philadelphia, so that he had to cross over into New
York—that hell upon earth. In 1614 a company of
merchants, having received permission from the States-

---

* An Anti-Slavery Society was formed in 1706. (*Vide* "Historical Sketch," ch. i.)

general, fitted out a squadron of several ships and sent them to trade to the country which Hudson had discovered. A rude fort was constructed on Manhattan Island, which was the beginning of the city of New York.

In 1643 the family of Anne Hutchinson and many others were massacred near New York, which threw the whole of New England in jeopardy and alarm.

In 1645 the brave Mohawks came to the rescue of the whites, and on the ground of the battery of New York "the tree of peace was planted and the tomahawk buried beneath its shade". In 1664 the profligate Charles II. granted the place to his brother, the Duke of York and Albany. Nichols took possession in the name of his master, and called the place New York. While the place was yet under the Dutch, Negro slavery was introduced about 1628. Later, the West India Company pledged itself to furnish the colonists with as many blacks as they conveniently could. In 1702 Queen Anne directed the governor of New York to " take special care that God Almighty be devoutly and duly served, and that the Royal African Company of England take especial care that the said Providence may have a constant and sufficient supply of merchantable Negroes at moderate rates ".

New York followed all the examples of the South in her barbarity to the Negro. In 1711 a slave market was created in Wall Street, where slaves of every description were sold; the following year, the Negro, the Quaker, and the Papist were a trinity of evil.

The Negro had neither family relations (for they lived together by common consent under the eaves of churches), school, nor property. Neglected in life, they were left to be buried in a common ditch after death. No wonder that they created a riot, burnt a house, and killed a number of white persons. And had it not been for the prompt assistance of the troops the city would have been burnt to ashes; and the world would have been rid of ex-convicts and gaol-birds, who excluded the testimony of a Negro in a court of law and extended their authority over the life and limb of a race whom they tore from their home and country to enrich themselves.

1741 marks the period of the Negro plot, second only to that of 1769 in England, started by that arch-hypocrite, Titus Oates. One tragedy was acted in the metropolis of the old country, the other in her new colony. One was instigated by a perjurer and hypocrite, the other by an indentured servant; one originated in hatred to the Roman Catholics, and the other in hatred to the Negro; one was a religious question, the other was both social and religious; but they both agreed on one point, namely, the kind of evidence upon which innocent men and women were convicted and tortured. Evidence was wrung from lips steeped with lies: characters who were made to bear false witness by legal authorities. This lying and imaginary plot caused severer measures to be taken to keep down Negroism in the city. Nevertheless, in 1781 an act was passed for raising two Negro regiments in New

York, to whom freedom was promised; after service in
the army for three years they were to be regularly discharged.   In 1799, after three failures, the legislature
of New York passed a bill for the gradual extinction of
slavery.   In 1821 we find New York enacting that
" no man of colour, unless he shall have been for three
years a citizen of this State and for one year next preceding any election, shall be seized and possessed of a freehold estate of 250 dollars over and above all debts and
encumbrances charged thereon, and shall have been
actually rated and paid a tax thereon, shall be entitled
to vote at any such election.   And no person of colour
shall be subjected to direct taxation unless he shall be
seized and possessed of such real estate as afore-
said."

In 1846, and again in 1850, a constitutional amend-
ment, conferring equal privileges upon the Negroes, was
voted down by a large majority.   In 1863 a request
was made to the governor of the State of New York
to enlist coloured troops, but the governor never found
time, nor had the good taste to answer the request.
In 1864, without any bounty as incentive, out of 9000
Negroes, 2300 pushed forward with the greatest
enthusiasm to the aid of their brethren in the Civil
War, amid the applause of the most aristocratic
citizens of New York as they marched in the military
procession to the steamers on their way to the South.
Hawkins merely passed through the city on his way
to Albany; as there was no railway, he had to go from
thence to Buffalo on the Erie Canal, which journey he

accomplished in about three weeks; it was a beautiful morn in July when the runaway landed at Buffalo.

Such was the hatred of the anti-slavery movement in 1843 that Fred. Douglas says when he visited Buffalo : " All along the Erie Canal from Albany there was apathy, indifference, aversion, and sometimes mobocratic spirit evinced ". On arriving at Buffalo he began inquiring for members of his race, as was natural for a Negro to do at a time when white men could never climb down, even in a place free from actual slavery, to associate with him. He was at once directed to the best-known Negro in the town, who happened to be proprietor of an hotel of the baser sort—a whisky den. But, instead of speaking to the boss, as he intended, he walked out of the place and betook himself to the street, where he sunned himself by the side of a house ; here he basked for more than an hour. Before there was much stir in the city, an old man approached him as he came out of his house. " Good-morning ! " " Good-morning, sir ! " the fugitive promptly replied, thinking a good Samaritan had turned up, but, as he was indisposed to say more, Hawkins asked him how far was it to Canada ? To his sad disappointment, the man, pointing towards the dense forest on the other side of the river, which did not appear to be a great way off, replied : " There it is ". The answer struck him like a thunderbolt, and he refused to believe the old man, as his notion of the Queen's Dominion had been quite different. For most slaves like himself believed that when they came in

sight of Canada everything would be bright and cheerful and metaphorically decked with gold; instead of
which, Hawkins could not even see a house nor
anything that had the least trace of life, or that men
lived in that part of the world—neither could the man
convince him of the fact that the place he was looking
at was really the hope and expectation of the slaves in
the South. The old man, observing his disappointment,
said: "Are you going there?"

"Yes."

"What are you going there for, my lad? The
people are all starving over there, and dying every
day, and wages are only ten cents a-day in that
country."

Of course, such a report only tended to discourage
the poor fellow much more than it would have otherwise done if he had had more than a few cents in his
pocket, plus a hungry stomach. The old man having
knocked all the life out of him with his pessimistic
report, Hawkins gave himself over to the tender mercy
of the sun's rays; there he stood the remainder of the
day, having neither tasted food nor drank water,
until the poor fellow became faint and sick. The
building against which he was standing was rather
an ancient affair, being very long and low, at the
far end of which there lived an old Negress, who was
kind enough to come out and beckoned him to her;
but the fear of being recaptured and want of food took
every cheerful ray out of his spirit. "Know thee not
that our present existence is a compound of sweets

and bitters? Why not be hopeful and look up when everything seems to be against thee?" Ah! but it is quite a different thing to be on the best side of trouble, to make one, who is troubled, feel that his iron-bound environments will give way in the near future to sympathy, love, and release. The poor black woman, true to the instincts of the noble nature of her race,* seeing that the faint, sicken, hungry fellow made no attempt to move, approached him a little closer, still beckoning. Finding himself sinking under the heat of the sun and want of food, he made a desperate effort, summoned his courage, shook off fear and went toward the good woman. Who can doubt that God had sent this friend?

> When through life's dewy fields we go,
>   With flowers on every side,
> Thou art our Father, and we know
>   Thou art our Guide.
>
> When some rough, thorny path we climb,
>   And hope has gone away,
> Yet Thou art with us, all the time,
>   By night and day.

"You are a stranger, are you not?" said the old dame.

"Yes."

"Where are you from?"

"Near Washington," was Walter's reply.

"Oh!" she said. "I am from Honey. And what is your name?"

* Mungo Park.

"Hawkins."

"Oh, dear! my name is Hawkins, too. Come in and make yourself at home; there is no one here but me."

Of course she claimed relationship. And why not? They might have been. But the iniquitous slave system made it almost impossible for parents to know their children, much less any distant relation.

"Then," continued the old woman, "are you a runaway?"

"Yes."

"And so am I. You must be someone related to me."

Oh, Fate! what must have been this woman's difficulty to get so far, seeing that Walter Hawkins had gone through so many perils to reach her house? What must have been her suffering, when a strong, robust fellow's sufferings were so great? What light—what a revelation eternity will make—will throw upon the life and adventures of hundreds of Negroes who tried to make good their escape from the curse of slavery!

"Ah!" she said, "you must be very hungry." There is none to sympathise, like one who has gone through like sorrow.

Hungry wasn't the name for the confusion that was going on inside the young fellow. Knowing he was in want of food, she got to work and made something ready for him to eat, and he ate as heartily as when he was in the train from Delaware to Philadelphia, carrying everything before him, or, as a friend of mine said when we got up from a table where we had had grouse set before us: "I ate grouse until I grew feathers". Having eaten a good, square meal, he told her all about himself, and she did the same, and in her house he found a home for three weeks.

"She gave him friendship of her graciousness." Kindness draws the child to the mother's bosom; in the father it first loves the benefactor, the guardian, and fosterer. Kindness attaches the foster-child to its foster-parents often with a fairer tie than that of blood; it binds the pupil to the teacher, and establishes between them a friendship and attachment that lasts unto the grave; it weaves the first threads of that fair bond that binds us not only "to our country," as De Wette said, but to strangers who befriend us when we are on the brink of despair.

CHAPTER VIII.

BUFFALO.

Privations, evils, trials of poor humanity—yet good! If it be
God's will that poor humanity should bear them, who
dares murmur? Ah, it consoles one for many things un-
alterable and inexplicable to stick by that old-fashioned
precept of Christian philosophy, that whatever cross we
carry is rough-hewn in heaven.
—HOLME LEE.

"BUFFALO is situated at the north-east end of Lake Erie.
It has altogether a commanding position as a place of
business, being at the western extremity of the Erie
Canal, and at the eastern termination of the navigation of those mighty lakes—Erie, Huron, and Michi-
gan. The city is partly built on high ground, and commands an extensive view of the lake, Niagara river,
and the Canadian shore. The main street is a very
handsome thoroughfare, more than two miles long,
and one hundred and twenty feet wide. There is a
pier, extending fifteen hundred feet, on the south side
of the mouth of Buffalo Creek, which forms the
harbour of Buffalo, and which constitutes a substantial breakwater for the protection of vessels from the
furious gales which the inhabitants occasionally experience." Buffalo being a busy, go-ahead city, its

trading facilities by the canal in connection with the
lake navigation made it a great commercial mart.
In 1840 its lake navigation had an extent of some
thousands of miles; its shipment included 639,633
barrels of flour, 883,100 bushels of wheat, 47,885
bushels of corn, 18,435 barrels of pork, 7027 of beef,
and 9008 of ashes. The tolls amounted to 410,100
dollars, or about one-third of the dues of the entire
canal. The population was nigh 20,000, and it was
well provided with hotels for the numerous travellers
who were passing through to the mighty inland seas
of America. Along the wharves were to be seen, and
more often heard, criers vociferating the names of the
different hotels—the clamour of a hundred voices, not
at all musical, in the distance—all anxious to take
passengers to different establishments. As the regula-
tions of the port forbade "runners" from boarding
the steamboats, these men would arrange themselves,
soldierlike, along the pier in a closely-packed mass;
each endeavoured to howl down the other in order
that he might get a subject. Buckingham says: "The
competition and vociferating were great enough at the
landing-places in the country, but it seemed to us that
Buffalo bore away the palm from all others in this
respect". Such then was the state of things when
Walter Hawkins arrived in the city.* It was busy
enough to make the fugitive feel that there was a
chance to get some employment; in this he was not

* Bishop Hawkins arrived in Buffalo about 1837.

disappointed, for by the assistance of his benefactress, who had given him friendship of her graciousness, he obtained a situation as waiter in one of the many hotels of the city. This was actually the first time in the man's life that he had a voice in the value of his labour. He began to work for himself at ten dollars per month, with a view to rise to fifteen, besides "tips"; he soon convinced the "boss" that he was worth the higher sum. Now the fugitive felt that his prospects were much brighter; the black clouds which had so long darkened his horizon would be scattered, and he who had been a slave would be every wit free.

> 'Tis liberty alone that gives the flower
> Of fleeting life its lustre and perfume,
> And we are weeds without it. All constraint,
> Except what wisdom lays on evil men,
> Is evil; hurts the faculties, impedes
> Their progress in the road of science; blinds
> The eyesight of discovery; and begets,
> In those that suffer it, a sordid mind; unfit
> To be the tenant of man's noble form.
> —COWPER.

Hathaway, who employed him as a waiter, was not a bad sort, for the time and country which produced him; he passed for a Christian on Sundays, but during the week he could be heard swearing like an old tar, when called out of his sleep to shorten sail; otherwise, he was inoffensive, except when put out. Of course there were many things to throw an hotel proprietor out of temper sometimes, yet he was very honest, when asleep. Hawkins got used to his terrible out-

bursts of "cussing" after a while, and quite made up
his mind to settle down in Buffalo as his own master,
working away for Hathaway and the almighty dollar.
While working in this hotel, Walter's curiosity to
learn to read and write began to take definite form ;
as there were no night schools which he could attend,
he utilised all his spare moments in practising to write
and spell at home. His great ambition was to be able
to read the Bible for himself, and to sign his own
name. More important still was his desire to know
whether what his spiritual fathers had told him was
true, for he had doubts. To use the Bishop's own
words : " I rather doubted what they had told me,
especially as to what I had to do, to obtain a seat in
the kitchen in heaven ". It strikes us as though the
Negro would score on his master, when he needed food,
when once the Negro got possession of the kitchen.

Slaves had not only been told that the kitchen had
been allotted to them, but to get even there it was necessary for them to submit to any cruel act of torture,
which tyrannical masters might inflict, without a murmur. The institution was divine, and either to run
away or retaliate when struck were acts which would
be disapproved by God, and thereby forfeit every claim
to admission into the kitchen. To verify these
statements from Scripture was his one desire. Thus
he divided his time in spelling, copying, and, as a
Methodist, attending class and prayer meetings among
his own race. As the Negroes in Buffalo had no place
of worship at this time, they were compelled to hold

meetings in each other's houses or in groves, as some
of them had done, and their kinsmen were then doing,
in every slave State in the Union. How like the Christians of apostolic times! It was not by choice that they
worshipped God in such places; and yet what better
place could they have? Where slavery did not exist its
prejudices did. They repeatedly tried to get a building, but bigotry and hatred conspired to, and verily
did, thwart their purpose; and when they did get a
site no one would trust them or be responsible for the
cost of building a church. Poor as the Negroes were
in Buffalo, they succeeded, by perseverance, hard
work, and with a leader like Hawkins, in knocking
up a wooden building capable of accommodating between two and three hundred people, and the chief
carpenter's service was afterwards secured as their first
minister. Thus Bishop Hawkins had the honour of
causing the first Methodist church to be built in Buffalo. He resided in the city for a little over three years.
By this time his brother, whom he met in Philadelphia,
had removed from thence to New Bedford, Mass. The
glowing accounts of the place which his brother sent
him made Walter feel discontented with Buffalo.
Moreover, he began to get tired of bachelordom; therefore, he contemplated getting married and taking his
departure to the Quaker town, where the black people
lived happier than in any of the places he had ever
heard of. Hawkins had made good money at Hathaway's Hotel in "tips," so that he had little need of
drawing much of his wages; besides, if he had, he did

not know what to do with it. Consequently he allowed
his employer to take care of his money for him—
about three hundred dollars ; which was saved, as he
thought, to start his married life upon. Having made
up his mind to take to himself a wife on the strength
of his savings, he went to his employer and presented
his bill for the amount. Of course Hawkins' own
mind was full of grand thoughts about the future,
never dreaming that there might be a slip between the
cup and the lip. To his sad disappointment the pious
knave took the bill from him, and, with a nasty sneer
on his face, said : " I have got an old hog in the pen,
you can have that for what I owe you " ; which reply
struck poor Hawkins like a thunderbolt. The fellow
was paralysed for the moment and dumb. Would this
pious prig have sneered at a white man who had worked
for him so many years and then taunt him by offering
his servant a hog, which was far more honest than
himself ? Would the thing, wrapped up in man's
clothing, insult one of his own colour in this fashion ?
Certainly not ! Any injustice could be heaped
upon a defenceless Negro, who had run away from
slavery, with the greatest impunity. Walter found out
too late that he was not the only man whom this
scoundrel had served like himself. For it was an old
trick of the descendant of an ex-convict to get runaway
Negroes into his service and then plunder them. What
was the poor fellow to do under the circumstance to
get his money ? for it was of no use him going to law
with a man who had nothing in his own name, and if

he had, there was little chance of a Negro beating a white man in a court of law, because of the one-sidedness of the administrators of the law. His only hope for satisfaction was in revenge, but "that thirsty dropsy of our soul is cruel". Besides, he would have stood no chance in the midst of the rabbles of Buffalo.

As he saw no hope of redressing his wrongs, he resolved to leave the impious villain and make a fresh start. With the few dollars he had by him he took to himself a wife, and shook the dust of cruel Buffalo from off his feet, and directed his steps to his brother at New Bedford, Mass. Disgusted with Hathaway's treatment, and disappointed with the city whose institutions were no better than the South, where he had spent his early life, he determined to quit its associations. Though free, his environments were cold, too cold for men whom custom had made slaves—a custom fortified by law, solidly bound together by pecuniary interests, upheld by political combinations, strongly cemented by colour prejudice, and still worse by the fear of letting the Negro feel that he was the equal of the bigots whom he served. But the time was drawing near, when oppression would find its level, like all other acts of injustice ; however much individuals resist the silent attacks of conscience as well as the appeal of reason, the time must come when tyranny's power must be broken. When Walter Hawkins was wandering from State to State, first hiding in a room, then flying before constables ; now in a train, then beating a hasty retreat from some real or imaginary

pursuer; now in a comfortable bed, then on a tramp;
now waiting in an hotel and then running to a place
where he thought he would enjoy absolute freedom
—an undercurrent was finding its way in American
society, which would one day move the country from
centre to circumference. Never in human history
were there such conflicts between right and might,
and between the supremacy of conscience and caste
prejudices. As there was not a shadow of hope for
the poor fugitive, he took his wife and set out for the
Quakers' town. Nevertheless, he had done some good
for his race in Buffalo, for he had organised a congregation of Negro Christians and built a church. He
had learnt to read and could now write his own name,
and, better still, he had secured a wife who would
share in his triumphs and sympathise with him in his
troubles. By building a church for his race he gave
them their first lesson in the art of government, and led
them to unite their forces as well as to utilise their
combined resources. As long as black people live in
Buffalo, Walter Hawkins' name will abide, as the one
man who first taught their ancestors that there was
strength in unity. Not a unity which breaks down
the limits and levels the peculiar characteristic of the
different Negro tribes that were thrown together in
America, but rather a unity, the result and product of
those very national varieties and antagonistic qualities,
which points to the realisation of those rights which
are the birthrights of every race.

CHAPTER IX

NEW BEDFORD.

God created the smile and the laugh, as well as the sigh and the
tear. The aspect of this life is stern—very stern. It is a
very superficial account of it which slurs over its grave
mystery, and refuses to hear its low, deep undertone of
anguish. But there is enough, from hour to hour, of
bright, sunny happiness to remind us that its Creator's
highest name is love.
—ROBERTSON.

NEW BEDFORD is about sixty miles from Boston,
Massachusetts. It was discovered and visited by English navigators nearly twenty years before the Pilgrim
Fathers landed on the rock at Plymouth, by Gosnold,
who commanded one of Raleigh's squadrons in his
early voyages to Virginia. He landed on the coast of
Massachusetts by pure accident, as he was of opinion
that a shorter route might be found to the continent
of America than that usually pursued by way of the
Canaries and the region of the trade winds, by keeping
farther to the north, and thus making the degree of
longitude shorter than near the equator. Gosnold
was commissioned, by royal authority it is supposed,
and with the concurrence of Raleigh himself, to make
such a voyage according to his own judgment. The
object of his voyage was to find some suitable place

farther north than the Chesapeake Bay for a new
settlement. Gosnold sailed from Falmouth, in Corn-
wall, on the 26th of March, 1602, in a small barque, the
whole equipage of which consisted of thirty-two persons, only eight of whom were mariners. After a passage of seven weeks, they sighted America in the lati-
tude of 43° north; here they were greatly surprised
by the appearance of a European-built boat containing
eight Indians, two or three of whom were wearing
European garments, which aroused their suspicion
and deterred them from landing in spite of the Indians'
entreaty, for they thought that some ship had been
driven ashore, the crew murdered, and the boat and
garments seized by the wild children of the land.
From thence they continued their course southerly
until they found themselves "embayed with a mighty
headland," within a league of which they anchored in
fifteen fathoms of water. Here they caught a great
quantity of cod-fish, from which circumstance they
named the promontory Cape Cod. Having weighed
anchor, they proceeded farther south, and on the 24th
of May, 1602, Gosnold crossed Buzzard's Bay and
discovered the inlet from the sea on which the towns
of New Bedford and Fairhaven are now seated. The
Indians received the strangers with open arms, for
" men, women, and children entertained Gosnold and
his crew with courteous kindness, giving them skins of
wild beasts, tobacco, turtles, hemp-coloured strings
(wampum) and such like things as they had about
them ". If these Indians could have foreseen the kind

of treatment they (seventy-four years after) received
from Colonel Church and his puppets they would have
made short work of the invaders.   In 1676 the gallant
colonel attacked the innocent Indians—in the very
neighbourhood where his ancestors were entertained
—and took many of them prisoners, and, to the disgrace of the government of the colony and horror of
the Indians, they were ordered to be sold as slaves.

In spite of Colonel Church's opposition to their
banishment, the government of the Pilgrim Fathers—
who had themselves fled from tyranny—sent the poor
Indians away and sold them as slaves at Bermuda.
Alas! for the inhumanity of those Pilgrim Fathers!
Methinks that people who had suffered as they, ought
to have been brim full of justice and kindness.   But
the "scales of earthly justice are not poised in their
quivering equilibrium by huge hundredweights, but by
infinitesimal grains, which need the most wary caution,
the most considerate patience and the most delicate
touch to arrange or readjust them"; so these
Fathers were too full of self-love to be kind to the
Indians, and too eager to make sure their own safety
to tolerate the presence of the children of the forest in
their midst; hence, either from revenge, fear, or it
might have been to strike terror into the Indians, that
they began the work of extermination.   "It is kindness
that makes life's capabilities blossom, and paints them
with their cheering lines, and endows them with their
invigorating fragrance.   Whether it waits on its supe-
riors, or ministers to its inferiors, or disports itself

with its equals, its work is marked by a prodigality
which the strictest discretion cannot blame." This
sort of kindness was either unknown or wilfully withheld from the Indians, by men who would have been
insulted, and verily were, when the Romanists regarded them not as Christians but heretics. We do
not know what the Papists meant by the term " here-
tic," but we believe that their conduct towards the
Indians has taken much lustre from their history in
New England. It is astonishing how " men driven
from their fatherland, not by earthly want, or by greed
of gold, or the lust of adventure, but by the fear of
God, and the zeal for a godly worship," could have been
so cruel to the natives of the land of their refuge.
How could they " glorify God and enjoy the presence
of their dearest friends," and be happy in their inhuman treatment of savages in the country they had
chosen to enjoy liberty, and to make a home, is
difficult to understand. These Puritans were good
men in their own country, while groaning under
the rigour of tyranny, but the moment they landed
in a new country, where they were " well weaned
from the delicate milk of the mother country, and
inured to the difficulties of a strange land," they were
not satisfied with making war upon a people who
received them as kindly as their barbarity allowed
them, but sold them into slavery. We do not forget
what good these Puritans had done and suffered for
liberty of speech, press, and conscience, but we cannot
help observing their brutality to a brave and capable

people, and this we are bound to notice since the work of extermination which these (otherwise) noble-minded men began is being carried on in the United States to this day.

The spot on which New Bedford stands was originally called Acushnett by the Indians; but, in 1765, one Joseph Rotch, a Quaker, removed thither from Nantucket, for the purpose of developing the whale fishery in this port. There he found that "the most substantial farmer on the spot was Joseph Russell, a descendant of the Russell after 'whom this house' was called. The place was converted into a garrison in 1676." This Russell was also the chief landowner. It being thought desirable that a new name should be given to the settlement, which was about to be made on "Acushnett" to distinguish it from the township of Dartmouth, of which it was a part, and Russell being almost the only landowner, Rotch jocosely called him the Duke of Bedford, from his being descended from the "house of Russell," and called the town Bedford also. The epithet "new" was subsequently added when it came to be discovered that there was already a place bearing that name. Some, however, think that the place was first called "Bideford" by the original voyagers, who gave the names of Devonshire and Cornish towns to the places as they discovered them. The first house was built in New Bedford by John Louden, in 1758; but not until several years after did other settlers make their home there. "The Indian wigwams, stumps of recently cleared trees, and

the anvils of the smiths, were all mingled together."
A good anecdote is told of the sagacity and wit of an
Indian. The governor of Rhode Island paid a visit to
New Bedford, and while dining with the Indian chief
in his farm-house he asked the savage : " How many
evil spirits he supposed there were ? " To which the
Indian replied : " Every ordinary man had one, but
great men must have two, as he had always observed
them to have more evil propensities than others". A
sarcastic remark which the governor would appreciate,
because he well knew the kind of treatment the settlers had administered, and were administering, to the
natives.

From its natural beauty and convenience of the
harbour, New Bedford was destined to become one
of the great seaport towns of North America. In
1767 the first ship was built and launched from the
edge of the forest which furnished the wood for her
construction, and made her first voyage to London
deep laden with a cargo of whale-oil. She was then
the property of Quaker Rotch, and was named the
" Dartmouth"; it was the same vessel which afterwards carried the cargo of tea from London to Boston
which was destroyed by being thrown into the harbour in the commotion which preceded the American
Revolution. At the beginning of the War of Independence New Bedford was the only port eastward of
the Chesapeake which was not in possession of the
British. Then it was that the inhabitants built a
fortress at the entrance of the harbour. They sent

out many privateers, and many prizes were brought into that port. The town was stormed, burnt, and plundered in 1778, when all the property was destroyed. In 1787 a tract of land, thirteen miles from north to south and four miles in breadth from east to west, was incorporated as the township of New Bedford. In 1796 a bridge was built across the arm of sea which divides Fairhaven from New Bedford, a mile in length, and a lighthouse was erected about the same time at the entrance of the harbour. The Society of Friends built their first meeting-house in 1785, but they used to assemble in their schoolroom previous to this. So rapidly did trade increase that in 1838 the first bank was established in New Bedford. From this period the progress proceeded apace with wealth, industry, and good taste; so that, by 1838, New Bedford ranked as the third port in importance of its tonnage in the Union—the order being New York, Boston, and New Bedford. They carried on an enormous trade in whale fishery, so that New Bedford alone furnished nearly half the number of ships and men employed by the whole country in the boldest and most enterprising branch of maritime production. Her ships could be seen round the east and west capes, cruising all over the Pacific Ocean, off the coast of California, and as far as the islands of Japan. All nations could be seen in the port of New Bedford, who were brought there by the ships that anchored in those distant countries while in search of whales.

After a residence of three years and a few months in

Buffalo, as we have said, Walter Hawkins left with his wife and took up his abode in the prosperous town of New Bedford, on the recommendation of his brother. Having arrived in the busy Quaker town, he looked about him for something to do ; but kept hotels at a respectable distance, as he was afraid lest there might be some more Hathaways acting as proprietor and swindling black men at the same time. Nor was he free in his own mind from any apprehension of being kidnapped ; for there were a gang of villains, whose organisation extended from New England to Virginia, who lived by kidnapping as many Negroes as they could and sold them in the South. At last he found employment, doing first one thing then another for a livelihood, as did also his wife. Having saved a little money, they resolved upon opening a small grocery establishment, in which they did well for a time ; but, not knowing much about business tactics, they found that, instead of it keeping them, they had to keep it, at a loss of their capital. The man was too kind-hearted to refuse his customers provisions when they had no money, and relied too much on their gene-rosity to pay when they received their cash. In fact, he trusted entirely to the honesty of his customers. For aught we can judge, they might have been as honest as himself, and would have paid him when they got well off. Whatever their intentions were, Hawkins had not sufficient reserved funds to endure such a panic as his might-be-honest customers brought upon his small business. Consequently, he had to put up the shutters, satisfy his own creditors—for it does not matter who owe us, our great concern is whom we owe — and conceive some new plan for making money without the risk of being fleeced by his creditors. Thus, with a peace of mind which comes from faithful labour for good ends, and a courage kindled by the flames of many adversities, he turned his attention towards farming. First, because he had been accustomed to it as a slave in Maryland; secondly, because he had lost heart by failing in business; and, thirdly, because there was, at this time, great inducement held out to black people to go to Garret Smith's land. With all these forces working upon his mind he straightway resolved on going, without even counting the cost of getting there or thinking about the privations he and his family might have to endure, and gathered up his belongings and bade farewell to New Bedford, after having been a citizen of the grand old commonwealth of this historic town of Massachusetts for a period of eight years, all of which were spent in Christian usefulness among the black people in New Bedford. For, besides labouring about the docks, lamp-lighting, etc., he had a class of seventy Negro men whom he met week by week, teaching them what he knew about the Bible, besides preaching to others the love of Christ to fallen humanity, and the unspeakable joy there is in Christian life.

CHAPTER X

LIFE AS A FARMER.

Nothing is so contagious as enthusiasm; it is the real allegory of the tale of Cerpheus: "It moves stones; it charms brutes. Enthusiasm is the genius of sincerity, and truth accomplishes no victories without it."
—BULWER LYTTON.

NOTHING but enthusiasm would have influenced a man like Hawkins, who was ignorant of the art of farming, to take his family, consisting of his wife and three children, from a town like New Bedford, which offered so many advantages to a black man, to dive in the backwoods, almost penniless, to start a new life. Nothing doubting, in company with some other families, they went into the State of New York to a place called Florence. Having arrived, they felt that their primary duty was to clear away a site and make provision for their bodily comfort. To secure this they plunged into the forest as quickly as possible, clearing everything before them. Then they built log-cabins, converted bark into money, and sent timber to the sawmills, besides keeping a large stock to burn during the cold season. So that when the wind began to proclaim the advent of winter they found themselves fairly well provided for, and, as their wants were neither many nor great, they were perfectly satisfied with the common necessaries of life. Hawkins himself was far better provided for than when he was a slave in Maryland. They managed to struggle comfortably through that bitter cold winter, much better than their highest anticipations gave them warrant.

Towards the summer Walter began to think how he could augment his funds. Finding himself so near the Sarratoga Springs, the thought occurred to him that he might turn over some ready money there. Sure enough he thought rightly. After having sown his crop he betook himself to the Springs, leaving his wife, who was a real helpmate to him, to look after affairs. For three or four months in the year this hard-working, good woman would attend to the farm without neglecting her duty to her children. As the fall advanced, Walter would leave Sarratoga and get home in time to reap his harvest. In this way they managed to keep the wolf from the door, besides putting by a little. But in the midst of prosperity—just as if a black man had no earthly right to any luxury, when everything bid fair towards compensating him for all his past misfortunes, and just when fate began to pour upon him some blessings for the vinegar and gall which the curse of slavery had made him drink—trouble came, not from potato blight, or a plague of locusts to devastate his crops, nor from any epidemic which threatened to break through and shatter his family circle—but as though the man was born to be disappointed and sentenced to life-long trouble, only to be relieved with enough pleasure for him to know what happiness was like : the Fugitive Slave Law which was passed in 1793, against the continuation of which the Negroes of Philadelphia had presented a memorial to Congress in January, 1800, a law which the memorialists said "subjected them to great inconvenience and severe persecutions" though freed men, and a law which gave considerable trouble in 1817-8. To quote Mr. Williams : "During the session of that year the old fugitive slave act was amended so as to make it more effective, and passed by a vote of eight-four to sixty-four in the Senate ; with several amendments and heated debates, it passed by a vote of seventeen to thirteen ; but, upon being returned to the House for concurrence, the northern members had heard from their constituents, and the bill was tabled, and its friends were powerless to get it up". By this same abominable law, which was demanded by the south, the northern members, either through fear or fraud, voted them the right to hunt slaves upon free soil. The law passed, and was approved on the 18th of September, 1850, while Walter Hawkins was prosecuting his laudable occupation as a farmer. The slave-holders knew that the nefarious system was on its last leg, and it was necessary for them to make one desperate struggle against the growing and ever-increasing power of the anti-slavery party. England had given the death-blow to the accursed traffic ; France had followed her example, and St. Domingo had cut the throats of its oppressors. The Yankees saw that the press was going solid against them; the abolitionists were gaining sympathy everywhere, and the Negroes themselves were becoming a real political force in the free States, therefore they felt that if they could recapture the slaves who had escaped into the free States they would at least delay the death-blow. Thus the act was to the man-stealer what a straw is to a drowning man, and it acted as a source of terror to men like Hawkins, who had gained their freedom by running away from their bondage. Nay more, the law did not merely put the fugitive in danger of being taken anywhere, but threatened to take the Negro who had been born free; for the white man had only to swear that such and such a man was his property, and, as his words would be more readily believed, it was not safe for either a full-blood Negro or mulatto to remain within its grasp. The people everywhere were thrown into a panic. What was Hawkins to do in the circumstance? He was no longer a man whose hat covered his family, and he could not skip off as he had done before. At first he thought he would stop and fight it out, but then, what if he was killed in the battle? What would become of his wife and children, who had not known what slavery meant? If he was taken away or killed there was a chance of them being taken south and sold on the auction block. What was the meaning of such a clause as the following: " That any person or persons who shall attempt to remove, or shall remove, from this State, *i.e.*, Ohio, or shall aid and assist in removing, contrary to the provisions of this act, any black or mulatto person or persons, without first proving, as hereinbefore directed . . . shall, on conviction thereof before any court having cognisance of the same, forfeit and pay the sum of one thousand dollars," etc.? when "no black or mulatto person or persons could be sworn or give evidence in any court of record or elsewhere in the State," etc.? It was thus that the fugitive law made every Negro distrust his safety in any State. No system of injustice died harder than slavery. This law made the heart of many a stalwart man quake and tremble. It was enough to make them cut the throat of every white man they met. What other race would have tolerated centuries of the same kind of wrongs and abide under the sting? I grieve to think that my race was so patient. Will the time ever come when our race will rise to the occasion and strike for the justice which has been kept from them, or will Providence redress the wrongs inflicted upon the innocent? We have suffered as no other people in the memory of man—suffered more than Greeks, Romans, Indians, and Jews. Oh, ye gods! will the day ever come when we shall have recompense for the murder, torture, and cruelty inflicted upon us and our fathers? Will heaven look on and not shed a tear for the millions who have gone in the spirit-world without a ray of light? How could the earth and seas drink the blood of so many men without crying shame and demanding punishment for their murder?

Looking at the past from where we now are, it seems

a miracle that human nature can inflict so much and suffer so much without war and bloodshed. Yet it did, and the Negro race must wait and see the salvation of a just God. Most assuredly if there is no future punishment there ought to be. While contemplating the destiny of his family under the renewal of the Fugitive Slave Law, Hawkins remembered that he had been told when he first arrived in Buffalo that no one could recapture a fugitive on the Canadian soil. But how could he break up the little home and tear himself away from the friends he had made in the desert place? Ah! liberty was too precious a prize to chance being recaptured. Sitting down and leaning his head in his hands, he began to picture to himself the miseries of confinement, and compared them with the probable difficulties of a new country. However, he concluded that it was better to enjoy his own liberty, as well as to secure the same for his wife and children, than to live in fear. He collected such things as were easy to carry away, and started with enough money to take them across the border. For he—

> Had heard that Queen Victoria said,
>   If slaves would all forsake
> Their native land of slavery
>   And go across the lake,
> That she was standing on the shore,
>   With arms extended wide,
> To give them all a peaceful home
>   Beyond the rolling tide.

By the Fugitive Slave Law, slaves became "privileged property". A northerner, suing in the South for a

stolen horse or other abstracted valuables, had to pay
his own expenses, whilst the costs of the planter, for
the recovery of his slave, were paid by the Federal
Treasury from the funds of the North as well as
the South. By threats of secession the South succeeded in gaining its object, so that any slave
" escaping from one State into another shall, in
consequence of any law or regulation therein, be
discharged from such service or labour, but shall
be delivered up on claim of the party to whom such
service or labour may be due ". The moment this
law came into force the southerners, thinking that
slavery was protected thereby, began to pursue their
slaves in the free States, which caused a great many
riots and much loss of life. Here is a very striking
case : A slave, who had absconded several years
from Baltimore, had settled in New York as a
mechanic. There he had married a beautiful quad-
roon, and lived happily in his humble station. Mr.
Reese, his former owner, though regarded as a pious
man, could, but did not, resist the inducement of
recovering his " property ". He had the man arrested
and brought before the court at New York. The wife
and children of the unhappy man followed him before
the judge. They clung to the prisoner, who was to
be separated from them probably for ever. They cried
while Mr. Busteed, the counsel for the plaintiff, stated
the case and appealed to the judge to enforce the
law which had become the pledge of the North to the
South, and the great tie of the Union, and therefore of

the prosperity of the States. The lawyer himself was moved by the heart-rending sight; and, to show his compassion with the woes of the poor woman who witnessed in tears the painful act of what went for "Justice," he peeled an orange and offered it to her. But how could she partake of it? It was not an orange she wanted, but her husband. Mr. Jay, the counsel for the defendant, objected, first, to the proceedings on technical grounds—for he saw that the case was desperate—and then appealed rather to the feelings than the law. At this Mr. Busteed became excited, rushed forward, and boxed the ears of his colleague in the open court. The judge was so shocked at his conduct that he forthwith withdrew from the court. When order was restored, the slave summarily delivered himself up to the counsel for the plaintiff, and tore himself away from his wife and children, who, crying and wailing, followed the carriage which took him off. It is, however, fair to add that Lawyer Busteed, having accomplished his duty as a citizen, endeavoured to do what he ought for humanity. It was a tragedy which acted strongly on the feelings of all who witnessed it, and on none more than the counsel for the plaintiff, who set to work, put his name down for one hundred dollars, and collected the necessary funds amongst his friends and other benevolent persons in New York, for the liberation of the slave, whom he recovered from his client. He brought him back to liberty, and restored him in about a fortnight to his distressed family. In all, pious old

Reese got, by the generosity of the public, about one thousand dollars. The scoundrel ought to have had the cat instead. We hope the ill-gained money did him no good. Anyhow, it was such cases as these which brought the horrors of slavery before the minds of the American public, and hastened the death of the system.

Walter Hawkins was perfectly right not to risk any such chance, for he might not have had such a benevolent lawyer to help him out of his difficulty. Once in Canada the Fugitive Slave Law was a dead letter so far as himself and all the Negroes who got there were concerned. There are a few stupid people yet who think that a religious slave had no right to run away; but surely it was as righteous an act as stealing a man from his country, and much more so. Hawkins and his family without further risk crossed the line singing :—

> " We are on our way to Canada,
> Where coloured men are free ".

Prince Albert wisely said that " freedom is an idea which can only be realised in a State which sets up laws modelled upon the divine laws of morality in the place of arbitrary caprice, and establishes a physical force to uphold those laws and carry them into practice. It is only in this way that freedom is able to pass into a condition in which it may exist without limitation, and where nothing *but itself* can impose limits upon it." It was a wise Providence which ordered the situation of Canada at a time when millions of people were groaning under the lash and extravagance of the United States' Government. Indeed, Canada was a sort of land of Canaan to the Negro. He sang, sighed, and longed to get there, as did the Jews for Zion, as they wept by the rivers of Babylon. In spite of its distance from the South, nothing but physical and brute force could prevent their striving to get there. What but the Providence of God can account for the fact that Washington and his contemporaries did not extend their dominion farther north?

CHAPTER XI

CANADA.

As that whole design was formed by me, I have a sort of paternal concern for the success of it.
—VISCOUNT BOLINGBROKE'S CORRESPONDENCE, vol i. 161.

SUCH was the utterance of the noble statesman who planned the conquest of Canada. It would never do to allow a statement like the above to appear without explaining that it was due to a bold design of Sir David Kirk and his two brothers, Louis and Thomas, to attempt the reduction of Canada in 1628. Thomas Kirk was commissioned to ascend the St. Lawrence, and Quebec received a summons to surrender. The garrison, which was destitute alike of provisions and military stores, had no hope but in the pride and daring of Champlain, its commander. His answer of proud defiance concealed his weakness, and the intimidated assailants withdrew. In 1629 the squadron of Kirk reappeared before the town, and found the garrison reduced to extreme suffering and on the verge of famine, in consequence of Richelieu not having sent supplies, thus the English were welcomed as deliverers. Favourable terms were demanded and promised, and Quebec capitulated. Thus eighty-three years before the conceited Bolingbroke penned his famous letter (1711), and one hundred and thirty years before the dashing enterprise of General Wolfe, England took possession of Quebec : indeed, " not a port in North America remained to France from Long Island to the Pole, and England was without a rival ". But Quebec was soon after restored to the French.

About daylight on the 13th day of September, 1759, General Wolfe—in whom Pitt confided the command against Quebec—provided with a choice army of 8000 men and a heavy train of artillery, leaped on the shore. When he saw the difficulty around him, he said to one who was near him : " I do not believe there is any possibility of getting up, but we *must* do our endeavour ". The rapidity of the stream was hurrying along the boats in which the soldiers sat. The shore was so shelving that it was almost impossible for them to climb up ; and it was lined with French sentinels, one of whom hailed the Englishmen : " Qui va là ? " and was answered by an English captain in French, " La France," as he was instructed to do so. " À quel régiment ? " redemanded the sentinel. " De la Reine," replied the captain. " Passe," said the sentinel. Escaping these dangers at the water's edge, they proceeded, though with their hearts in their boots, to scale the precipice, pulling themselves up first by roots, then by branches of trees and the projecting rocks in their way. The party who reached the heights first secured a small battery, with which they covered the remaining army, who ascended the summits in safety. Montcalm was thunderstruck. "It can only be a small party come to burn a few houses," said he.

There, on the lofty plateau, which commands one of the most magnificent outlooks which nature has formed, the gallant Britishers, drawn in a highly advantageous position, were safe until the following morning, when they were discovered by the French. At the same time Montcalm learned with profound surprise and regret the advantage which the English had gained upon him. And, having left his strong position, he crossed the St. Charles; and, displaying his lines of battle, intrepidly led on the attack. In the heat of the terrible engagement which followed both commanders were mortally wounded. General Wolfe received three wounds before he fell. He was quickly removed from the field, but he watched the battle with intense anxiety. Being faint by the loss of blood, he reclined his languid head upon the supporting arm of an officer. "They fly! they fly!" cried someone. "Who fly?" asked the dying general. "The enemy," was the reply. "Then I die content," said the brave warrior, and gave up the ghost. No less marked was the heroism of the French general, who, when he was told that his wound was mortal, said: "I shall die, not live, to see the surrender of Quebec". Although the war continued twelve months longer, the French finally surrendered all their possessions in Canada on the 8th of September, 1760. In 1762 peace was signed at Paris, by which France ceded to Great Britain all the conquests that she had made in North America.

There is no doubt but that Canada is a country of much value. In spite of its rigid cold climate, it affords beautiful landscape and a variety of sceneries; it can boast of the finest river in the extreme north of America. The timber trade, the original occupation of the people, is still of great commercial value, although it is fast giving way to agriculture, dairy farming, and cattle raising. Fisheries are also an extensive branch of industry. The country abounds in minerals, but these are scarcely developed; petroleum is produced in large quantities. The land, as a rule, is fertile, and produces all the varieties of cereal, fruits, roots, etc. There is no doubt but what there is an immense future for Canada; as is evident from the fact that every year more and more capital is being employed in her great manufacturing centres. Already Montreal and Toronto command a vast system of communication by canal and railway, both with Canada and the eastern and western parts of the United States; and we may add that education is practically free, and children have the chance of acquiring the highest education at a moderate cost.

It is more than forty years since Walter Hawkins took up his traps, left the United States, and made his home in the city of Toronto, where his sister had been living for some years after she left New Bedford. He arrived in Toronto a poor man, having comparatively nothing to face the winter which was fast coming on. But he had been too often on his beam-ends to be overcome by this new difficulty; so he forthwith

turned his hand to the first thing he could find.
Once on British soil, there was now no fear of being
re-captured. To use the Bishop's own words: "I was
protected by the British lion, so that there was no
fear of my being taken from his watchful eyes and
powerful claws". His intense trust in God never left
him. "I knew," he says, "there was One above who
would never leave me nor forsake me." Here he soon
made friends and joined the Methodist Church, in
which the whites prevailed, there being no Negro congregation in the city at that time. This he could not
have done unless they were quite different from "the
mean whites" whom he had left behind him in Yankeeland. At this time the Negro population was very
limited. He soon became an active and useful member in the church; by which means he won the affec-
tions of the white people, and was raised to the
position of a local preacher among them. As the
churches were scattered, he had to travel through
primeval forests to preach to the black population of
the district. When he did not lose himself, he was
so mangled by mosquitoes that when he arrived in
church he looked more like one who had been
fighting than a preacher of the Gospel. Everywhere
he went he was cordially received, and well
treated by the congregations, white and black,
thus making his labour sweet. While he was away on
Sundays his wife, who had materially helped him in
all his troubles, would gather what few coloured children there were in the neighbourhood together, and

hold a Sunday School in their own house. Sometimes she would tramp miles with him; at other times the good people would give them a lift in their traps. Gradually, by the kindness of the Canadian people, they were able to restore the home which they were compelled to break up in the States on account of the Fugitive Slave Law. They would even supply them with provisions until his prospects began to look more hopeful and bright. His children, too, seemed quite happy in their new home as they romped among the trees and flowers in the summer with a glee born of freedom. What a blessed thing is liberty! His home was now his own; his "bread was provided and his water was sure". In fact, they had plenty of the comforts of life; their health was good, and their minds were at rest. So that their sleep was such as they never could have enjoyed in the United States. A few years after his settlement in Toronto the conference of the British Methodist Episcopal Church met in that place, and he was induced to make application to join them as a preacher. This he resolved to do, because he could see that there was an immense field for work to be done among his race, and that it could be better done by the aid and influence of a powerful body behind him than without. The association not having sufficient men, they readily received his papers, and, being satisfied that he was the kind of man to do the work, the conference there and then appointed him to the Brentford circuit, which was about one hundred miles in length. But how was he to get to the place?

He had come to Toronto a perfect stranger, and nearly penniless, so that it took all he could earn to build up his home ; in fact, he had not made quite enough to keep his family, and had therefore to get into debt. He felt that it would hardly be the correct thing to commence his ministry owing any money : he ought at least to start fair and square as a minister of Christ and a fellow-labourer of one who said : " Owe no man anything ". The people, too, considered that no minister should owe money even if his family were starving—a standard of morality we have no objection to, but they ought not to have allowed the family of their minister to so feel the pinch of poverty as to be tempted to get into debt. Just when he was reasoning the matter to himself, a friend of his informed him that the provincial fair was coming on, and " you might make some cash by having a tent and provide people with food as long as it lasts ". This struck Hawkins as a happy suggestion, and forthwith he began to make his tent. He worked day and night to get it ready, so that he might have a good pitch—and a real good pitch, too, he got. The fair began in fine form. It was a glorious bright morning, and everybody was ready to spend money at games of chance, or anything else. Hawkins soon found his tent brimful of hungry customers ready to eat him out, but he was ripe for the occasion, and the first day passed off well for his business. Having cleared away his things, and got his establishment ready for the next day, the poor man retired for the night, weary with his long, laborious day's work. Between the middle of the night and the small hours of the morning he heard a crash at the door of his tent. Surely, thought he, it couldn't be a lot of hungry people knocking him up to be fed. Just then another tremendous crash came against the door, down it fell, and in came a crowd, crushing in the tent like an angry wave, armed with clubs as if they were about to attack a regiment of wild Indians. Presently the rabble made for the donkey-breakfast on which he was resting his weary limbs, and began to walk into him, as though he had murdered some white man, on whose behalf they were about to take vengeance for the crime. They knocked him senseless, dragged him out on the grass, and left him for dead. But what had the man done to merit the usage which he received from the hands of the ruffians? The villains thought the man had made a lot of money, and that it was an easier job for them to rob him than to work. So they fell upon him and spoiled him of what he had. How long the man lay in a state of semi-consciousness, and when these scoundrels took their departure, no one knew. But when Walter Hawkins came to himself—or what was left of him—he found himself in the house of an old man with whom he was acquainted. This dear old man acted the part of the good Samaritan, for he sent Hawkins home in a conveyance just as he was, torn and tattered. The tent he had knocked up of rough boards was as badly used as himself, for the rabble, having got what they wanted—but much less than they expected—completely wrecked the shanty, leaving things scattered all over the grass. Of course, the cowardly trick made matters much worse for the man, who was trying to get out of debt in order that he might begin his laudable calling with a clear conscience that he owed " no man anything ". Alas ! this horrid incident was a fearful drawback for him and his family, for they had stretched every nerve to get the outfit for the tent ; and, having lost all, he found himself almost worse than he was before he was offered the ministry at Brentford. At this critical juncture friends offered to share his troubles, and gave his family sufficient of their bounty to keep them from starving. We cannot speak too highly of the kindness of the people towards the Hawkinses. They were as different from the Yankee whites as day and night ; in fact, all the while the head of the family was ill they almost entirely depended upon the charity of the good people for sustenance. And before the unfortunate man recovered one of his children died from the shock which he received on seeing his father brought home in rags and covered with bloodstains. How soon after the sunshine of prosperity one may be followed with storms of ill-fortune is clearly seen from the rugged life—and, indeed, all through the career— of Walter Hawkins.

CHAPTER XII

THE FIRST CIRCUIT.

There need be no disappointed ambition. If a man were to set
before himself a true aim in life, and to work definitely
for it, no envy or jealousy, if he considered that it mattered
not whether he did a great thing, or someone else did it—
nature's only concern being that it should be done; no
grief from loss of fortune, if he estimated at its true value
that which fortune can give him and that which it can
never give him; no wounded self-love, if he learned well
the lesson of life—self-renunciation.

—JOHN RUSKIN.

YET he hoped against hope, as he took a turn for the
better and was on the way to recovery from his
dreadful mangling. The doctor ordered him not to go
to his appointment for another six months, lest he
might lose his reason. But how could any man who
was at all active see his family struggling, to make a
living for themselves and their father, without himself
trying to help them? When a man is incapable, of
course, loving children will show their father every
respect; and this is just what the younger Hawkinses
did do, until their father got well enough to start to
his ministerial duties at Brentford, Ontario. Where
the money came from for him to go, he did not know;
but it came, and he considered it to be a token, that

(132)

God approved his appointment to that circuit. On arriving at his journey's end he found that his work would not be easy, for the church was stripped and the people scattered through the conduct and mismanagement of his predecessor. But Hawkins was too well acquainted with uphill work to shake his head at the condition of things which stared him in the face, so he made up his mind to strive and do something that would glorify God and bless humanity; he, therefore, plunged headlong into his work, visiting from door to door, talked to and entreated the people to try and open the church again; but they, not knowing the character of the man, and having been bitten by the previous preacher, were a long time in getting up their zeal to the point where the new minister required it. However, he persevered and pegged away at them until gradually he succeeded in winning them one after another. By-and-by he got a few around him who formed the nucleus for him to open the church. Forthwith he re-established the regular Sunday services, but he had more often to preach outside, as they flocked in larger numbers than he anticipated, to listen to him. Those who took the trouble to hear him preach slowly began to put confidence in the integrity and earnestness of their minister, and were finally induced to make a collection for him, but not until he had spent some months among them and won his spurs. The first collection amounted to twelve dollars (£2 10s.), which he sent to his wife by one of the Brentford pietists, who took the liberty of going into partnership with Mrs.

Hawkins. This unprincipled man promised to refund the same at an early date, but it never came off. So the money was lost to them at a time when they could ill spare it. While Preacher Hawkins was toiling up-country and gathering the people who had been so long without a shepherd, his good wife was toiling to keep the body and soul of her family together. In order to do this, she ofttimes had to leave her children without a fire and very little food to go and do a day's work to make sure of the rent. Poor noble soul! What a charming chapter it would be if all the acts of real heroism and self-sacrifice of every nation were written! ah, written as the acts were accomplished, not merely stating the fact that such and such persons did certain things, but how they did them. This (it seems to me) would convince men quicker than anything could, and show the world that human nature is the same everywhere and in every age.

> Ye are all human; yon broad moon gives light
> To millions who the self-same likeness wear;
> Even while I speak, beneath this very night,
> Their thoughts flow on like ours in sadness or delight.
> —ANON.

The noble woman, Mrs. Hawkins, did many acts of true heroism, but nothing so touchingly self-sacrificing as during the time her husband was up-country with no fixed salary, and when he could not send her money, to relieve her of financial embarrassment. Their eldest son, now twelve years of age, set to work to help his mother by selling newspapers and doing a little light portering. Of course he earned very little, but it helped to make things more cheerful for the family. Besides this, the little fellow would gather wood and make himself generally useful when his mother was hard at work and from home. Help from a boy like this worked wonders in his mother's heart! As time went on the Rev. Walter Hawkins, as he was then, began to feel he should be where his family were or they where he was. Moreover, he had been long enough in the circuit to test their appreciation of his labour. Nay, if the people saw them, thought he, they might more readily pay him a fixed salary, so that he might support his children as all respectable men ought. This he told his congregation, who had by this time much more confidence in him, and forthwith they saw, as he did, and probably felt the same thing before he had spoken, only it would not do to tell their minister. Anyhow, they put their belief into practice and their sympathy into action, raised the necessary funds among themselves in order that he might pay the fares of his family from Toronto to Hamilton. Indeed, one member even offered to go to Hamilton and bring them and their luggage from that place to Brentford, provided he had not too much goods, a proviso that needed no answer if the good man had known that the family had not enough money to buy food, much less could they afford to spend money on such luxuries as expensive furniture. Accordingly they went for them, and brought the bare necessaries of household goods; the rest, Mrs. Hawkins was bound to sell for what she could get for them. Again the family met together, after many vicissitudes, at Brentford, to start life under new circumstances and with new environments. Soon after the family arrived, a revival broke out in the town, and many new members were added to the church; by which means the minister got a little more generous support, which was very much needed, as sickness laid many of the family low and created fresh difficulties and additional expenses. The Fugitive Slave Law, of which we have spoken, drove more black people into Canada, which gave Mr. Hawkins more anxiety for their bodily and spiritual well-being. Besides preaching at the head of the circuit, he had to travel day and night under very trying circumstances. Often he had to go out in the morning after a light breakfast, and walk, talk, pray, and sing a whole day before having any dinner. In some villages he had all that to do on an empty stomach, as the people had barely enough for themselves, far less to give anything away. Indeed, the man could not find it in his heart to take from people who ran away from slavery as penniless as he himself was when he made good his escape to Philadelphia. The poor wretches, on entering Canada, had to dive straight away into the wild woods to make a home for themselves as best they could. Not only had they to clear the land that had been given to them, but they were bound to work for the farmers around to get bread for their families to subsist upon, until such time as their own crops grew, and were reaped to turn into ready money. What could a poor Methodist minister do in the midst of such poverty which stared him in the face? How little can we, who live in a country much more favourable than theirs, imagine what must have been the sufferings of a minister and his flock in a new country at such a time! What aching hearts, hungry stomachs, and destitution must have reigned in their midst! Bishop Hawkins often looks back on those dreary days, saying: " I would get a quarter of a dollar, sometimes a half, and maybe a little meat, flour, or potatoes, just as it might happen "; and yet he felt happier than when he was a slave. He would travel around his circuit once in four weeks, proclaiming the message of salvation to his race, under conditions far different to those of old Preacher Proctor. That alone was something to thank God for. His income was then about one dollar, or four shillings and twopence, for four weeks' hard labour. Though hard, the work was pleasant. Fortunately for him and his family, the people who lived immediately around them, in the circuit—Brentford— were much better off, and were therefore able to, and did, supply them with some of their provisions. They made a sort of free-will offering for his ministerial labours among them occasionally.

Amid all his troubles, none seemed to have affected Bishop Hawkins more at that time than to leave his dying son to go on one of those four weeks' ministerial journeys. While away from home, he received a message that the boy was dead.

Naturally, he felt bound to return; to get home he had to walk eight miles to the nearest railway station. Once there, he did not stop to discuss the morality of travelling without a railway ticket—so he jumped into the train. Sometime after the train left the station, the conductor went round to examine the tickets, only to find the Rev. Walter Hawkins without his ticket. Then the man demanded his fare, to which he replied: "I have got no money, my son is dead, and I want to get home". Dead or alive, the man wanted the fare, or else he must get out at the next station. So he offered the conductor his watch for security. After a moment's thought, the man took it, we suppose acting on the principle that his watch was a more reliable entity to pledge than his word. On their arrival at Brentford, as fate would have it, he met a sympathising friend, who was always interested in him, and who said to him: "Job," as he was accustomed to call his Negro friend, "have you heard the sad news?" "Yes," said Mr. Hawkins. "How did you get here?" asked the man. "I have pledged my watch to the conductor for my fare," was Job's reply. The man said no more, but ran to the train, paid the conductor, and brought back the watch. What a blessing he was not in Yankeeland! He would have been whipped as a common robber, sure! This white friend did not only redeem his watch, but went with him to his house, to see what else he could do for his friend. Thus by his aid, as well as the kindness of his neighbours, he managed to provide a decent burial for

his son. Well might Helps say : " Since men are so
miserable, always say a kind word when you can, and
do a kind action when you can ; it may come in so
opportunely—it may save a man from despair ". In
this case one cannot tell what Walter Hawkins would
have done, but for the prompt and kind action of that
friend at a time when he most needed one.

> An arm of aid to the weak,
>   A friendly hand to the friendless ;
> Kind words so short to speak,
>   But whose echo is endless.
> The world is wide, these things are small ;
> They may be nothing, but they may be all.
>   —LORD HOUGHTON.

Beyond Brentford, the people were too poor to give
their minister one good meal when he went among
them. Indeed, they lived in small log-houses. The
churches were little places built of the same materials
as their dwellings. Ofttimes the reverend minister
held services in total darkness. " One evening," says
the Bishop, " I went to take the service in one of my
outlying churches. As I approached the place I could
hear my congregation singing, quite half-a-mile away,
before I got to the place." It is only those who have
heard American Negroes singing their quaint melodies
that can imagine the enthusiasm they throw into
them. On his arrival, he was astonished to find the
hut in absolute darkness. At another place where he
was preaching, one old man got so excited that he
spat in his (the preacher's) hat, totally ignorant of
what he was doing ; another man took it into his head

to sing all the time the preacher was speaking, regardless of the comfort of any other person present. At one place the Bishop had to preach in a hut in which his congregation smoked their sausages in a mixture of tobacco and wood-smoke. The Bishop said the smoke was so dense and disagreeable that, before he had finished preaching, he was both sick and blind, so much that he had to go outside for a breath of fresh air. When it was time to go to bed, his host showed him a bedroom, with the same kind of furniture that the slave-holders gave the slaves down south. All the same, he slept on the floor and awoke the next morning quite sore. At another place, where he went to preach, the people thought they would have a light on the subject. So they got a tallow candle and cut it in three pieces, and stuck them on the sides of the cabin, so that the Bishop was compelled to talk against the light of the pieces of candle, in order that they might not be in darkness before the service was closed. Then arose the difficulty of finding him a bed. After a consultation among the members, one man offered to take the minister to his house. On arriving at the establishment, his hostess began to provide a supper, which was made of buckwheat flour and water, baked on the lid of the stove. After eating a few mouthfuls of the cake and sausages (cured in tobacco smoke), the tired man was glad to sleep on the bed provided for him on the hard floor. For two long years he went about this circuit, with not half the comfort of an ordinary London missionary, and, in spite of the trouble, poverty, and hardships he encountered, he took pleasure in the work of preaching to his race, who were real objects of pity indeed. Everywhere he went, he saw the evil effects of the institution of slavery on the manners and morals of the people ; nay, oft-times he felt that it would have been more satisfactory to labour among a Pagan race, rather than a people whose notion of religion was an imperfect knowledge of Christianity. But this was more the fault of those who had enslaved them than their own, consequently all his sympathy went out to them ; and at the end of his two years' ministry he could see a marked improvement upon their moral and spiritual life. Here the Bishop was thoroughly convinced that the civilisation of the most degraded race rested on Christianity, that it could only be raised by Christianity, and only be maintained by Christianity ; not the dogma of theologians and the ceremonies of a church, but the Christianity of Christ, " who His own self bore our sins in His own body on the tree, that we, being dead to sin, might live unto righteousness," " by whose stripes we are healed ". Many will rise up on the last · day and praise God for having raised Walter Hawkins to preach the religion of His Christ among them, for, though their bodies were free, such was their love of sin, and the power it had over them, that only Almightiness itself could and did make them free from its awful consequences.

Chapter XIII.

ST. CATHARINES.

Man can have strength of character only as he is capable of controlling his faculties, of choosing a rational end: and, in its pursuit, of holding fast to his integrity against all the might of external nature.

—Mark Hopkins.

At the expiration of two years from his appointment as a minister of the Brentford circuit, the conference from whom he had received his mandate met at St. Catharines, which he attended and gave an account of his stewardship. The conference must have thought that a change of place had been well earned by the Rev. Walter Hawkins—and well they might, for he had succeeded in pulling the churches in the Brentford circuit together, reclaimed many who had fallen away from the faith—though they nominally clung to what was left of a church—and added many new members to the circuit. Besides, he had done good service for the physical and moral wholesomeness of his race, ofttimes going without comfort himself. The conference, feeling that its faithful minister needed a change, appointed him to St. Catharines circuit, the place in which it was then sitting. As his wife was unwilling to remove again after so short a time, he left her and

(142)

their children in the old circuit at Brentford, returning home once every three months. While he was attending to the work of his ministry, his wife was plodding away as she had always done. Some time after his new appointment she saved enough to buy a cow and a few chickens, whereby she was able to sell both milk and eggs. Mr. Hawkins found himself well looked after in St. Catharines, and things generally began to be quite comfortable; indeed, they soon bought another cow. When he went home, there was no more of that story of hardship which greeted him on his six weeks' tour through his old circuit. No more hungry children crying for bread, and none of those deep, loud sighs from his wife. The home was very comfortably furnished, plenty of food in it, wife cheerful, and the eldest son, who had done a good deal of light portering, etc., had got a good situation, and helped his parents all the more. Sure enough patience and perseverance were bringing their own reward.

> We have not wings, we cannot soar,
> But we have feet to scale and climb
> By slow degrees, by more and more,
> The cloudy summits of our time.

The hardships which Bishop Hawkins had undergone made an impression of a serious character upon him, in mind and body, but his wife and eldest son heroically shared his grief with great fortitude and pluck; the latter especially almost lost his elementary education for his heroism in his endeavour to work and help to support his younger brothers and sisters. "The man, woman or boy who can give up dreaming and go to his daily realities, who can smother down his heart, its love and woe, take to hard work of his hand, who defies fate, and, if he must die, dies fighting to the last—that person is life's best hero." Work, wait, win! seemed to have been the family's motto, for there was a happy co-operation always existing between children and parents; they verily loved to bear each other's burden. But how could this sympathy exist? but for the untiring energy and self-sacrifice of the head, who knew how to suffer and inspire confidence and devotion into those for whom he had to work. Walter Hawkins had passed through the furnace in slavery; he was made to bear up against terrible odds while making good his escape, and his life, up to the time of his getting married, was one long series of trial, which did not improve when he increased his responsibility by taking a wife. Fortunately for him, the good woman had sympathy for him, or how could he have borne the uphill struggles of Florence, and the awful fatigue which the work of his first circuit involved? Well did Whipple say: " Heroism is no extempore work of transient impulse—a rocket rushing fretfully up to the darkness, but which, after a moment's insulting radiance, is ruthlessly swallowed up—but a steady fire, which darts forth tongues of flames; it is no sparkling epigram of action, but a luminous epic of character ". This is really the kind of heroism we seem to see in Walter Hawkins, and it is the same spirit which his children inherited, and kindled such a flame of devotion towards him in the hearts of those among whom he laboured. His work at St. Catharines was highly appreciated by everybody—his power of organising, his simplicity, his childlike trust in God and humility, won old and young; indeed, it would have been difficult to find a man at that time with so little education who could have accomplished so much under similar circumstances.

After serving the people of St. Catharines two years, he was removed from thence to Dresden circuit, near Chatham; at the expiration of other two years the conference sent him to Chatham. For four or five years previous to his appointment to the Chatham circuit, Mr. Hawkins was contemplating buying a house and a piece of land which he could call his own, so that when old age came upon him and his good wife they would have where to lay their heads. When he took up his abode in Chatham, he began to look around for a site upon which he intended to build the house of his dream. With his usual patience he awaited his opportunity, and at last the site was found, and considerable time was allowed him to pay for it before he could secure the freehold. He had been a farm labourer and farmer, a waiter, lamplighter, grocer and light porter——why could he not be a landowner, builder, and minister? In most of his other undertakings he was not required to lay down much money : now, however, there was a large sum to put down as a first instalment, but he had only ten dollars to call his own. His son, upon whom he could depend on a push, stepped in and helped him with the amount required. The land being secured, he went straight ahead with his building project, without waiting for a more favourable opportunity—which might never have come. "The man," said J. B. Gough, "who waits for some seventh wave to toss him on dry land will find that the seventh wave is a long time coming. You can commit no greater folly than to sit by the roadside until someone comes along and invites you to ride with him to wealth or influence." This move proved to have been both wise and good, for the moment he commenced to build he got lots of friends to come to his assistance, for both the members of his church, and people outside his congregation, gave or did something for the carrying out of his scheme. Sure enough, many hands made light work, for some helped by giving a day's work, others gave a few dollars, some in one way and others just as was most convenient to them. It is evident that the Chatham people had learnt that the true spirit of helpfulness consisted in searching out for some individual life that they could aid and encourage to bear burdens that otherwise might have crushed out all hope. What with the help he received from friends, his own energy, and his family's exertions, they managed to push on the work, and made sure of their house before the winter of 1866.

At the close of his ministry at Chatham, the conference sent him to Amhurstbury; there he found the people in a very low state of spirituality—poor, and with very indifferent places to worship in. Like his first circuit, Mr. Hawkins was obliged to hold services in the open air, in places where the dwelling-houses were too small to accommodate the large number of people who flocked to hear him. So small indeed were some of the log-cabins that the quarterly meetings were held outside. For two years he struggled on in the poverty-stricken circuit of Amhurstbury, on very small pay, and that which he did get was mostly spent upon the poor of his circuit. With a hope for better things, and that confidence in the future which never forsook him, he continued his ministration with marked success. By the close of his two years' ministry he succeeded in pulling the circuit together, increased the membership, and raised a better tone of spirituality among the members, and inspired a Christian brotherliness which made them try to find opportunities and outlets to bless others. Not only did he kindle in them a consideration that did not merely concern itself about other men's souls, and helped them to make the present more livable, but he taught them a Christianity which springs in the heart from love and devotion to Christ, and runs through all the commonest rounds and minor parts of their daily lives.

From Amhurstbury Mr. Hawkins returned to his favourite circuit—St. Catharines—which was at this time considered among the Methodists to be the best place for a preacher in the whole of Canada : because the people were for the most part pretty well-to-do, industrious, and generous. This time he took his wife and family with him. If we could but foresee our fate, it is certain we would be slow to follow our inclinations whither they would lead us. The return to St. Catharines was by no means so full of pleasure as it was with pain, both to himself and to the temporary loss of the churches in the province, for he had not quite settled down in the place before three of his children fell ill and died. "Death strikes down the innocent young; for every fragile form from which he lets the panting spirit free, a hundred virtues arise, in shapes of mercy, charity and love, to walk the world and bless it. For every tear that sorrowing mortals shed on such green graves, some good is born, some gentler nature comes. In the destroyer's steps there springs up bright creations that defy his power, and his dark path becomes a ray of light to heaven." (Charles Dickens.)

This sad circumstance fell upon Mr. Hawkins like a hurricane; for though friends rallied around him, and bore the expense of taking their remains to Chatham, where they were interred, the loss of so many at a single stroke completely brought the strong man to the ground—indeed, almost hurried a useful man into eternity. Alas! death has no regard for the bloom of youth any more than the wrinkles of the aged, and does not discriminate between the man of God and the man of sin; at his gaze all are made to tremble. The poor man broke down completely, and had to give up his work as an active minister; he, therefore, placed himself upon the superannuation list of ministers, as the shock quite incapacitated him for twelve months.

There can be little doubt but that the high pressure at which Mr. Hawkins had been working for years past had so affected his constitution that the sudden shock of the loss of his children laid him low in 1868. In England, even at that time, when a Methodist minister was superannuated he was allowed some financial help from the conference. But it was not so in that part of Canada; they could not give, because they had no money to spare. After absolute rest for twelve months, Mr. Hawkins rallied, and gradually began to regain his strength. At this point his white brethren, seeing that he was yet unfit to resume his ministerial duties, advised him to raise a band of singers— like those jubilee singers who visited this country years ago—and they promised to employ them in their various churches. Mr. Hawkins set to work and gathered a choir together; but, as he had no money to go to his first engagement, he had to fall back upon the generosity of his friend, Mr. Isaac Holden, who supplied the money with which he made a start. In the meantime, his wife, a son, and daughter opened a small shop, which they managed with better tact than the old people had done at New Bedford. The singing tour was a financial success; and on their return, not only was Mr. Hawkins once more himself, but he actually realised sufficient money to free his property from the debt which was hanging over it, and once more resumed his labours among the black population in the land of their adoption.

"One thing experience teaches: that life brings no

benediction for those who take it easily. The harvest cannot be reaped until the soil has been deeply ploughed and freely harrowed. 'Learn to suffer and be strong,' says the poet; and certain it is that without suffering there can be no strength. Not, indeed, that suffering is or makes strength, but that it evokes the latent powers, and arouses into action the energies that would have otherwise lain ingloriously supine. The discipline of life is a necessary prelude to the victory of life, and all that is finest, purest, and noblest in human nature is called forth by the presence of want, disappointment, pain, opposition and injustice. Difficulties can be conquered only by decision; obstacles can be removed only by arduous effort. These test our manhood, and at the same time confirm our self-control."

CHAPTER XIV

MADE A BISHOP.

THE Rev. Walter Hawkins' recovery and return into the regular ministry was hailed with general rejoicing and thanksgiving to Almighty God by the Negro population of the whole province, as during his retirement they were like sheep without a shepherd. Certainly their hopes were not at all disappointed, for he forthwith plunged into the work with a zeal which it would have been difficult for anyone to surpass. The churches had got into debts and difficulties, which he made it his first business to free them from, working night and day, might and main, in the name of the Lord, knowing and believing that He who had done so much for him in the past was able and would bring him and his people out of all their troubles, to rejoice in God their Saviour. "In this," said Mr. Hawkins, "my faith has not deceived me, for God has helped us to see our way out of all the difficulties we were in, and I have every confidence in His future guidance."

The Methodist Church in Canada, of which Mr. Hawkins was a minister, was part and parcel of the American Methodist Episcopal Church in the United States. But by a convention held in 1856 the Canadian portion separated from the mother church, and called itself the British Methodist Episcopal Church of Canada, under which name it confined its operations mainly among the coloured population. In the year 1882, when Bishop Dizney presided over the Church, an attempt was made by him to transfer the establish· ment to the supervision of the American Church for reasons which we cannot discuss. But this the people resisted (1st) on the ground of the Bishop attempting to do so without their united consent, and (2nd) because the people could not tolerate any Yankee government. But beyond these two reasons they remembered that when the United States' Government, by her Fugitive Slave Law, had driven the Negroes pall mall from the States, the Yankees winked at the slave-holders shooting down those who would not submit to the tyranny of slavery, and hunted others who had taken refuge in the swamps of the malarial South ; then it was that Canada gave them shelter and her Queen protected them. Thus, as a church, they desired to abide under the British Government, as they said : " This country and this government are good enough for us ". Ah ! England has no more faithful subjects anywhere than the Negroes and their children to whom her Canadian possession gave protection when the cowardly Yankee government refused physical and religious liberty to the Negro.

Against the handing over policy there was no stronger opponent than Walter Hawkins. He would have nothing to do with Yankeeism ; for, though the Negro was sometimes insulted in Canada, there was a

genuineness about the people which was impossible to
find in the States. They had had enough of Yankee
bounce, intolerance, and hardship in the past, and
abundant experience of caste prejudice to hand over
their congregation and all their property to the Yankee
Eagle. Besides, the white people were too well dis-
posed to them, and they had much more liberty than
they could ever hope for from the Negro-hating Yankees
to forsake the government of their choice. Indeed,
such is the Canadian Negroes' love for their Queen and
country that it will ever be impossible for them to act
in any way that would show a sign of ungratefulness
or ingratitude.

This was the spirit which prompted the members of
the British Methodist Episcopal Church to cling to
Canada and despise the temptation of joining hands
with the American Episcopalians. From 1856 to
1886 the Rev. Walter Hawkins laboured incessantly
to keep up the influence of the Church among his
people, so that we can understand somewhat the feelings of the convention which met at Windsor, Ontario,
in 1886, and selected the one man who remained loyal
and led the opposition in securing the best interests of
their Church.

Now that Bishop Dizney failed to carry the Church
as a body, and hand them over to the Yankees, his
only alternative was to retire, which he did, so that
the Bishopric became vacant; and now the convention
felt that their gratitude was due to Mr. Hawkins,
which they expressed by selecting him as their

Superintendent or Bishop for a term of four years. Mr. Hawkins, feeling that his education did not fit him for that post, at first refused, but it was useless, as they unanimously carried that he should take the office, which he, with some reluctance, did, and a right good Bishop too he made. Indeed, he gave such general satisfaction that he was re-elected in 1890. That a man who was born, and spent over a quarter of a century of his life, as a slave, and whose education was so limited, should be chosen as a Bishop, can only be accounted for, from his power over men, his influence with God, his power of organising, and his natural goodness.

The Reverend gentleman was never more surprised in the whole of his long life than when he was chosen to preside over the destiny of the Church he had so faithfully served; for, besides the consciousness of his inability, he was already advanced in years. However, with that courage and cheerfulness which marked his long career, he put his hand to the plough, putting forth his best endeavour to further the best interests of the Church whose fortune lay so near his heart. Certain it is that the Bishop neither sought the praise of men nor his own glory in accepting the office, for he tells us that his average income has never exceeded £40 per annum (200 dollars) for the last forty years. His self-denial, humility, and Christian character are known throughout the Province of Ontario. Soon after his re-election it was proposed that he should set sail for England, to which end testimonials were given him

by men of every calling in the town and neighbourhood where he resided for years. Here is one from a
dealer in grain : " This is to certify that I have known
Bishop Hawkins twenty years, and can testify to his
worth and ability as a Christian minister. He has a
happy way of presenting the truth of the Holy
Scriptures, and a power of applying them possessed
by very few. As a conductor of ' song services ' he
has no equal, particularly in his inimitable ' Nearer my
home to-day '. As a citizen, though differing in
nationality, his wise counsel and his true Christian
character make him a welcome visitor in our homes.
We join with many in wishing him God-speed in his
labour of love.—N. J. BOGART, Chatham, Ontario."

Another from a lawyer of high reputation in Chatham gives the reason why he was so popular, as well as
the motive which helped to influence him to cross the
Atlantic : "This is to certify that I have known the Rev.
Walter Hawkins during the past thirty years as a
Presiding Elder and Superintendent or Bishop of the
British Methodist Episcopal Church. He is a man of
sterling integrity and irreproachable Christian character, endowed with fair natural abilities, sound judgment, and indomitable courage. He set his face in
uncompromising opposition against an attempt made a
few years ago by self-interested parties to alienate the
property of his Church, and to transfer it, together
with its membership, to a foreign jurisdiction, and
thus extinguish in one transaction the honourable
name and accumulated efforts of his people for nearly

half a century. That the attempt proved abortive, and resulted only in the detaching of a few small congregations, but with the conservation of the name and property of the British Methodist Episcopal Church, is *due to his tact and business capacity, combined with his ardent zeal for the work of God and for the prosperity of his people.*"

To champion the cause he had at heart, and to achieve this laudable success, material resources were likewise needed, so that he found it necessary *to pledge his name, his credit, and his provision for old age* in such a manner that a heavy weight of pecuniary indebtedness still rests on him in his declining years. With all this burden resting upon him, Bishop Hawkins neither worried nor fretted about it; his confidence in God never failed, for he believed that a way would be opened for him to get himself and the Church out of financial difficulties.

About the last week of September, 1890, the general conference of the Methodist Church in Canada received Bishop Hawkins and the Rev. Mr. Minton as delegates from the British Methodist Episcopal Church. "They both," said the correspondent of the *Methodist Times,* " are as black as ebony. One was their Bishop, who is known and beloved all over the Dominion. Twice did he fairly electrify the conference with his pathos and simple eloquence." At this meeting Bishop Hawkins delivered the following touching and telling speech :—

" Mr. President," said Bishop Hawkins, with an

accent and a pronunciation instantly recalling dear
old Uncle Tom—" Mr. President and "—here he
paused a moment, his lips trembling—" will you suffer
me to call you brothers?" The pathos of this would
have melted a heart of stone. " Yes, yes," burst from
the conference, like the voice of one man. " Thank
God," said the black Bishop, simply. It was a grand
moment. Many of the ladies in the gallery put their
handkerchiefs to their eyes. " You let me call you
brothers in Christ. It seems like a dream Here I am
in this beautiful church " (looking slowly round the
building), " and in the presence of the best intellects
in the country. You were born in all the advantages
and refinements of Christian civilisation. I was born
a slave." (Many found it hard to retain their com-
posure.) "I have heard that heaven is a beautiful
place; I can well believe it; I must be near heaven
now. (Applause and laughter.) Yes, it seems just
like a dream to be standing here. You are indeed in
the midst of every elevating influence; I come from
the auction block, an' dunno most how I got here. I
am a little blacker than you are, but "—here he
paused, and placed his hand on his heart; his eyes
grew moist—"but my soul is whiter than snow,
washed in the blood of the Lamb sixty years ago.
(Prolonged applause.) We are on a level, as far as
Christianity is concerned, and I am looking forward
to a time when complexion will be done away with.
(Applause and laughter.) I am a little darker; but
we're one in Christ Jesus. (Applause.) I remember

when I first heard that a Negro might have a soul, and that, if he were good to his master and mistress, he might get into the kitchen of heaven ; but I propose to go into the parlour of heaven with the president and the brethren." (Loud applause and laughter.)

"I suppose," said the Chairman, " we needed that little gleam of sunshine—(laughter)—and I'm glad so stalwart a brother as Dr. Williams has the floor, for I don't know anybody else who could so well bring the meeting to order." (Laughter.)

The following is the account, as it appeared in the same paper, of the more official visit made by the coloured men a subsequent day to the conference. There was a glorious time with Bishop Hawkins. That beautiful church of St. James will never ring with louder plaudits, will never witness a scene of greater enthusiasm, of more heartfelt emotion. The simple pathos of the Bishop melted every heart. His quaint humour convulsed the staidest man in the conference. Doctors and professors, owning its power, went down before it. But it was his singing that made the eye moist, and put a lump in the throat, and provoked hurricanes of applause that almost shook the building; and a general waving of handkerchiefs, from the Chairman (who is generally several degrees cooler than ice-water) to the timidest young lady in the gallery, and a violent blowing of noses throughout the house that made it just good to be there, and to see it all, and to share in it. First, the Bishop presented the greeting of his Church. "As I said yester-

day, brethren, it is almost like a dream. I never saw
such a beautiful church as this. I never saw such a
wonderful conference as this. I feel so lifted up that
I almost forget that I am black—feels like as if I
dunno whether I'm black or not. I have been insulted
in this city on account of my colour, though you have
received me like Christian gentlemen. (Applause.)
But I don't think my colour makes any difference to God.
(Applause.) Well, brethren, I come to you as a child of
God, having got the blessing of salvation sixty-eight
years ago, 'way down thar in the South. Ah, it was dark
then ! No privileges then. It was ten o'clock at night.
It was over the fence, away to the woods, one mile, two
mile, five mile, ten mile, to hear about Jesus. I became His child. And it has been better all the time
since. Better as I grow older. This is the happiest
day of my life. The way has often been rough and
dark. I have had a circuit of 100 miles to travel with
my legs for a horse—(laughter)—getting 100 dollars
a-year, with a large family to keep, often without food
for a whole day at a time ; but I loved my dark
brethren, and I went amongst them, and did what
you cannot do—I unlocked the door of their hearts
with a key which you could never get, and I sowed
the seed there. (Loud applause.) It was hard work ;
but I had the marching orders from the Master.
(Applause.) Now, my mind travels back to the time
when there was not a spot in North America where
the black man was free, and I think of my own early
days ; but if I once begin I'd keep you too long.

(Cries of 'No, no,' 'Tell us about your slavery days,' etc.) Well, then, everything was dark, and we heard that in Canada there was freedom for the slave. I thought Canada was behind the sun. (Laughter.) I didn't know the east from the west, the north from the south. But I got there, and I was free. (Loud applause.) I put myself under the paw of the British lion—(prolonged applause)— and when you're under the paw of the lion, and he gives a growl at your enemies, you're safe. The Queen of England—God bless her !—('Amen ') — the best woman that ever wore a crown or swayed a sceptre—(loud applause)— the Queen of England meets the Negro the moment he touches British soil—(prolonged applause and great enthusiasm) — and that's why I am here to-day. (Applause.) They wanted to transfer us to the American Church, but this country and this government are good enough for me. (Applause.) You made a great union some time ago. God prosper it. You did not take us in. (Laughter.) We are still willing to be taken in—upon conditions. We would want to have our own conference and our own rules, for you could not manage that. (Laughter.) But we preach the same Gospel, we have the same ordinances ; and I hope to live to see the day (for I'm as strong as I ever was, and didn't Enoch walk with God for 300 years ?) when we shall be one in name as we are one in faith. Our Church is not a great Church ; but all the same we don't want you to drag us into a union. We are doing a work for God, and preaching a free salvation ; and, if

there never be a union here on earth, I expect to meet
President Carman in heaven, where we will shake
hands, and say, as we see all the members of our
churches on the eternal shore: 'We helped to bring
these to Jesus'. Thank God for the happy thought.
(Loud applause.) I was on the mountain to-day; but
I was never nearer heaven than this moment. Deep
down in my soul I thank you for the way you have received me." (Loud applause.)

The Bishop's companion followed, and when he
sat down Dr. Douglas rose and said: "We want to
hear Bishop Hawkins sing". ("Yes, yes," "Sing,"
etc.)

"Will Bishop Hawkins sing 'I'm Redeemed'?"
said Dr. Douglas.

"If I can get the key," said the Bishop, amidst
laughter, "I'll sing 'Nearer my home'." He got the
key, and his soft, rich voice put a crooning lilt into the
music, and he closed his eyes, and gently swayed his
body, and waved his arms, and abandoned himself to
an ecstatic motion, which reached every heart in the
conference.

"Sing the chorus," said the Bishop. "We can all
sing it, for aren't we all going to the same heavenly
home? We may never met on earth again :—

> " I'm nearer my home,
>   I'm nearer my home,
>   I'm nearer my home, to-day,
>   I'm nearer my home, where Jesus has gone,
>   I'm nearer my home to-day."

The Chairman took off his spectacles and sang it. The venerable Dr. M'Mullen, the representative of the British conference, found himself singing and swaying with the rhythm; about five hundred voices, above and below, sang that chorus with a volume of energy and feeling that swept every tittle of the conventional clean out into the street.

" Now, I'll sing," said the Bishop, "' On my way to Canada'. This is the earthly home. But it was heaven to me in the old days, and many a time this song cheered my heart, for it seemed to anticipate heaven."

" On my way to Canada " represents the slave flying from the bloodhounds. He flees through wood and marsh until, on the other side of the lake, he sees the Queen of England standing with outstretched arms to receive him. The Bishop put his whole soul into this piece. A tide of emotion swept over him which glorified his poor old black, wrinkled face; his eyes became lustrous, his lips trembled ; he raised himself, held his hands over his head, and sang with extraordinary energy :—

> " I'm on my way to Canada,
> Where the coloured man is free ".

The contagion spread over the house. Roar after roar of applause burst from the conference. 'Twas a thrilling scene.

" I move that we take up a collection for Brother Hawkins," said Dr. Douglas.

" A collection," "a collection," was the cry. " Well, get the hat going," said the Chairman, wiping his eyes.

" A collection," he continued, "is a wonderfully cooling process."   (Laughter.)

But that collection amounted to ninety-two dollars, and every man and woman in the house put something into the hat.

Dr. Douglas wanted to hear " I'm Redeemed," but the Bishop found he couldn't sing it.   Brother Winter sang "The Land of Beulah".   He has a high tenor ; and the Bishop came in now and then with a soft, lilting tone.

The conference then passed a resolution, expressing its interest in the British Episcopal Methodist Church, and the coloured delegates withdrew.—REPRINTED FROM *The Methodist Times*, October 30, 1890.

CHAPTER XV

IN ENGLAND.

SUCH a speech from such a man forthwith induced an enterprising agent to write to the Bishop, inviting him to come to England, and offering him, among other things, a warm English welcome. The Bishop submitted the communication to his elders and friends, who advised him to go and state the case of his people to the British public, whom they thought would assist him materially. Before sailing with his devoted wife, whom he felt bound to take with him, the following letters are a few of the recommendations he received—besides the two we have already given—from the Canadian people.

"I take great pleasure in certifying that I have known Bishop Hawkins, of the British Methodist Episcopal Church in Canada, for a number of years past, and that his reputation as a minister of the Gospel and as a citizen has always been of the highest character. And I desire to add that this my testimony is, I feel positive, that of every citizen of this town of Chatham who has a knowledge in any degree of his Christianlike character, and I confidently recommend him to any and all with whom he may communicate during his mission abroad.

"JOHN TISSIMAN, Town-Clerk,

"Chatham, Ontario."

" My Dear Bishop,

" Allow me to congratulate you most sincerely upon your elevation to the high office of a Bishopric in your church. I need hardly say that I, in conjunction with your other numerous friends, wish you ' God-speed' in the noble work you have undertaken. Wishing you a pleasant voyage, and with kindest regards to your devoted wife,

" Believe me,

" Yours very sincerely,

" H. J. Patteson,

" Pres., Board of Trade, and

" Ex-Mayor of Chatham, Ontario."

" I have known the Rev. Walter Hawkins for the last sixteen years, and have great pleasure in certifying him to be a godly man, worthy of the respect and confidence of all Christian people, and trust that he will meet with great success in behalf of the British Methodist Episcopal Church, the prosperity of which in the name of God is so dear to his heart.

" Respectfully given,

" William Ward, Dresden, Ontario,

" Late of Norfolk, England."

" Chatham, 13*th Feb.*, 1891.

" I have known Bishop Hawkins for the last ten years, and have much pleasure in testifying to his stainless reputation and high Christian character.

Living in the town where the Bishop has resided for the past twenty years, I gladly testify to the esteem, the confidence, and the honour in which he is generally held by his fellow-citizens. I have yet to hear the first disparaging word spoken of him by anyone. He is a useful citizen, a devoted Christian, and an eminently successful minister; possessing an influence almost unlimited among his own people, his services are in demand and greatly appreciated by all the churches. I cordially commend him to the confidence and love of all Christian people.

"J. W. Annis, Pastor, and

"Chairman of Chatham District."

"Sarnia, 31st *Jan.*, 1891.

"This is to certify that I have known the Rev. Elder Hawkins for about fifteen years, and have had him with me on country, village, town and city work, and he has given satisfaction alike in all places. He is good, and to me a man who fits in wherever duty calls him. Personally, I esteem him very highly and love him as a brother. I have always found him a Christian gentleman. His presence always commands a large audience with us, as he is both eloquent and good. I commend him to all Christian people as a man and a brother in Jesus Christ.

"Thomas Cullen, Pastor."

"30th *Jan.*, 1891.

"To those Christians in England whom it may concern. This is to certify that for many years I have known Bishop Hawkins, of the British Methodist Episcopal Church in Canada. I can testify to his high reputation as a Christian man, to his fervent piety, his gracious influence in the churches that he has served as Pastor, Presiding Elder, and Bishop, to his manly common-sense and special ability to present with fitness and power the blessed truths of the Gospel; his power of song, though advanced age now rests upon him ; his brow abides with the inspiration of former years.

" He was welcomed as a representative by the last general conference, and his address and singing will never be forgotten. We commend him to the care of the Master whom he serves in crossing the ocean, and to the united confidence of the Christian churches throughout the motherland. All that know the dear and honoured saint will pray that his mission may be crowned with abundant blessing.

" George Douglas, Principal,

" Wesleyan Theological College,

" Montreal."

" The Rev. Elder Hawkins, of the British Methodist Episcopal Church in Canada, was received by the Methodist Church of Canada as a fraternal delegate at its last session, held in this city of Montreal in September, 1890. After an address from Elder Hawkins, the following resolution was unanimously adopted by the general conference and seconded in its journals. Resolved—' That we have listened with pleasure to the greetings of the British Methodist Episcopal Church in Canada, and to the interesting addresses of the Rev. W. Hawkins and the Rev. T. W. Minton, the representatives of that church to this conference. We do not forget that during the stirring times in the history of this country our coloured brethren were faithful to our institutions and loyal to the British Crown.

" ' We beg to assure these honoured brethren of our deep interest in the prosperity of their church, and wish them God-speed in their noble work of saving souls and advancing the best interests of the Church of Christ.'

" The address of Elder Hawkins before the conference awakened deep feeling, and won for him the esteem and affection of all who were present.

" S. T. HUESTIS,

" Secretary of the General Conference,

" Methodist Church."

Bishop Hawkins is a strong total abstainer, and an ardent temperance reformer, so that when the " Dominion Alliance " for the total suppression of the liquor traffic knew that he was about to sail for England they caused their correspondent secretary to write the following letter :—

" The Rev. Walter Hawkins is general superintendent of the British Methodist Episcopal Church in Canada. He is a Christian gentleman and an earnest advocate of the cause of temperance and prohibition. As such I have very much pleasure in respectfully recommending him to our prohibition co-workers in the motherland, which he is about to visit.

"F. S. SPENCE."

As Bishop Hawkins made no effort to come over to England, he says : "The Lord directed me to cross the Atlantic"; and here he has found more friends than he ever expected. Indeed, before he left the shores of Canada, he was well known to the Methodists in this country, besides the general public who saw the announcement in the daily papers that he had actually set sail for these shores. He arrived at Liverpool early in the spring of 1891, and there was no doubt about the kind of reception he met with in that city of many nations. The illustrious Charles Garrett was among the first to give him a warm welcome to England. As the following letters will give a better idea of how the Bishop was received in England, we will quote them.

"22 BALMORAL ROAD, TANFIELD, LIVERPOOL.

"Bishop Hawkins had a most enthusiastic reception on Wednesday last in Brunswick Chapel. The place was densely crowded, and the assembly deeply interested, while, for an hour and three quarters, he related his experiences as a slave, and his remarkable escape from slavery. His singing, too, was a special feature of the evening, which greatly charmed the people.

"The collection for his work was something between £20 and £30.

"W. MIDDLETON."

The Rev. Charles Garrett wrote :—

" Bishop Hawkins spent two days with us last week, and thoroughly captivated our people.   His humour, pathos, and strong common-sense were irresistible, and all our circuits are anxious to have a visit from him before his return.   He is 'a grand old man,' and I trust his visit to England will be a blessing to many."

From Liverpool Bishop Hawkins went to London, and spoke at the Wesley Centenary Memorial Meeting ; and, on the 11th of March, Dr. T. B. Stephenson, now President of the Wesleyan Conference, wrote the following letter :—

" REV. AND DEAR SIR,

" On behalf of the Committee of the Wesley Centenary, I beg to thank you most cordially for the great service you rendered our cause by speaking at the meeting of 6th March.   You will, I am sure, rejoice with us that signal blessing has rested upon the services.

" I am, Rev. and Dear Sir,

" For Self and Colleagues,

" Yours very truly,

" T. B. STEPHENSON.

" Rev. Bishop Hawkins."

A vast number of letters have been sent to the Bishop, besides the reports of newspapers all over the land, speaking in the highest terms of him.   He had a splendid reception at the British Temperance League, and spoke at their annual meeting at Exeter Hall, when (the Lord Bishop of London presided) he made a very favourable impression upon the audience. As a speaker on the platform, the Bishop must be heard to appreciate what is said of him on both sides of the Atlantic. We well remember his speech at Grosvenor House, the London residence of His Grace the Duke of Westminster, at the fourth anniversary of the " United Committee for the Prevention of the Demoralisation of Native Races by the Liquor Traffic". There was a grand array of honourables, baronets, divines, a colonial governor, Hindoos, Negroes, and a crowd of ladies and gentlemen ; and His Grace himself presided over the meeting.

Bishop Hawkins, who seconded the resolution, said : " My Lord Duke, I find myself where I never expected to find myself. I can hardly realise it when I go back in my own mind to my past condition; and when I stand here to-day, and witness and listen to what I have seen and heard, I am almost ready to say it is a dream. My soul is filled beyond any way of expressing my feelings. Why, the word ' My Lord Duke,' I did not know the meaning of it. (Laughter.) I could not tell whether it was a man or what it was. (Loud laughter, in which the Chairman heartily joined.) I don't know what to say. It affords me great pleasure, and is an honour beyond description, to be present at this grand meeting. Ladies and gentlemen, I wish I could say what I want to say, but there is something that springs up in my throat and chokes me, so that I can hardly speak. When I received an invitation to come here, I said to my wife : 'I don't think it is true'. I read something here—'second resolution'—'presided over by His Grace the Duke'; but it is so, I find it is true. I am certain that it will send joy into the hearts of my brothers on the other side of the Atlantic when they get the news that you have received me as a Christian gentleman and elder, leader of a great army of temperance workers. As long as you live we will follow you, and the work can be accomplished when such as yourself and the gentlemen around you say : 'Go forward ; the work must be done'. It will be done. (Cheers.) I see no reason for doubting it. Now, my brother who has just sat down—am I right in calling him brother?—(cries of 'Yes')—another step up the ladder—my brother has referred to God and Christ. Without their help no association or society in the world can stop the drink traffic in Africa. But with their help we can do it. I stand here eighty years of age ; but I am looking forward to the day when drink shall be driven out of the country. (Cheers.) When the members of the English Church and the Presbyterians and others become one, the drink is gone. (Cheers.) They are a power in the world to destroy this drink. I was glad to hear it was not England that carried the whisky to the Africans, but the whisky men in England who love drink and money more than they love men and lives. (Cheers.) We are trying in Canada to push forward

this great battle ; we are appealing to the legislators
to enact a law to drive the drink out of our land. I
have heard one of your legislators who are taking
steps to help the committee to remove this curse.
When it gets into the hands of the legislative body
and the Church of God, it will not stand ; it must go.
(Cheers.) I will not detain you by any more remarks
to-day. Wherever I go I will help the committee to
rouse the nations to drive out the drink, that Africa
may be saved. It makes one sick to think of it.
People don't understand it. Missionaries tell us they
have seen men and women and children dying from
the drink. Let each one of us start anew to-day ; let
each one of us take a part in the work ; let each one
of us go to the help of the weak against the mighty—
not only in Africa, but in England. (Cheers.) Walk
your streets ; oh, what shame ! Fine-looking women,
well-dressed women, some of them wives and mothers
—you may see them in your streets reeling with drink.
The whisky that is sent into Africa—give it to a common dog, and it would kill it. (Cheers and laughter.)
I don't wonder the men can't stand it ; I don't wonder
it should be found in Africa whilst you have it at
home. Remove it from England, and then say to your
neighbours : ' Here, follow our example '. (Cheers.)
I hope there will be a law that will banish these
miserable sights from our town streets and village
lanes, that the country will be Christianised in every
sense of the word, that God will bless this committee, and that every one of us will live to see the

day when the work it is doing will be fully accomplished." (Cheers.)

To say that his speech was well received is saying little.   We well remember the duchess sitting right in front the platform gazing in his face, when her face beamed as the Bishop made use of some of those quaint expressions which can never be put upon paper.   In fact, everybody was delighted, not so much with what he said as how he put it.

As we have before intimated, one must hear the Bishop to appreciate his peculiar style of oratory. His keen wit, his biting sarcasm, and apt as well as quaint sayings, impress one with the idea that, if he had been taken when young, he would have been a man whom any nation or age would be proud to call its own.   But not even his speech on that occasion approached the lecture we heard him deliver, on his " Escape from Slavery," for humour, pathos, and irony.   The people were sometimes on the verge of shedding tears, then convulsed with laughter, now clapping ; then a deadly silence pervaded the whole building as he told the unvarnished tale of slave life. He finished his lecture with his song : " I'm bound for Canada ".

In private Bishop Hawkins is somewhat retiring, but very agreeable; and when you get him on the track he tells some splendid stories.   He is a hearty laugher; his singing, too, is remarkable for his age. He never fails to impress you with his profound religious feelings, and his implicit confidence in God ;

there is no cant about him, for he tells you straight
exactly what he thinks when you press him for his
opinion. If he had lived in the reign of Charles I. we
think he would have been a Royalist, such is his intense reverence for our sovereign. He is always ready
to speak about his race, whose future destiny hangs
heavily upon him, especially in Africa. " Yes," he
once cried from the pulpit, " I would go to Africa
to-morrow if the Lord sent me."

Bishop Hawkins is a man of average height; and,
in spite of his great age, hardly stoops. His face re-
minds one of kindness, firmness, and goodness. He
has no superfluity of flesh, and never had ; indeed, he
is all bones and muscles. To look at him one cannot
help thinking how such a man could have gone
through so much ! But for his manly character he
never could have. He never takes a step to do anything without thinking over it, and taking his wife
into his confidence. No one can spend an hour with
him without profit. His anxiety for winning souls for
Christ is intense. His theology is as universal as St.
Luke.

The *Christian* says : " The Bishop is an emotional
preacher, after the type of others of his race. Pathos
and humour are unaffected, but form a strong feature
of his discourse. His sense of religious exercise
allows of heart-searching and soul-moving elements.
He tells of an influential and well-to-do minister who,
after many years of labour, said : ' I would give all I
have if I could recall one occasion on which my

preaching had caused a tear to flow'. He is privileged to look back upon an experience quite different, having seen men convicted of sin and converted to God as a result of his work."

Bishop Hawkins has made many friends in England, and we sincerely hope that the object for which he came will be fully realised. He has done his race good both in Canada and in England ; and, although we have not long known the grand old saint, we feel, as well as wish, it were in our power to do more than put this sketch of his long and eventful life together. We trust that his sanctity, firmness, good temper, and patience (which have won laurels for him in his persevering efforts for the spiritual and moral elevation of his race) will influence the younger generation of the sons of Africa wherever his life is read.